HUMPHREY BOGART

take it & like it

jonathan coe

BLOOMSBURY

HUMPHREY BOGART

take it & like it

jonathan coe

BLOOMSBURY

791.43

C2 143892 99

First published in Great Britain 1991
Bloomsbury Publishing Limited, 2 Soho Square, London W1V 5DE

Copyright © 1991 by Jonathan Coe

The moral right of the author has been asserted

A CIP catalogue record for this book
is available from the British Library

ISBN 0-7475-0657-4

10 9 8 7 6 5 4 3 2 1

Designed by Bradbury and Williams

Picture research by Juliet Brightmore

Typeset by SX Composing Limited, Rayleigh, Essex
Printed by New Interlitho spa, Milan, Italy

CONTENTS

INTRODUCTION

Humphrey Bogart is ancient history. Within movie terms, that is, since the industry has only been going for about ninety years and he has been dead for more than a third of that time. Cultish worship of his films and personality has become less prevalent – it was at its height in the mid-1960s – and the truck-loads of books that appeared in its wake have all slowly been allowed to go out of print. It is getting to the point, in fact, where we can start thinking about his career more objectively.

In the years since his death our feelings about acting in the cinema have changed. The assumption now is that the most conscientious film stars are those who subsume their identities into their screen roles: Robert De Niro stuffing himself with pasta in order to put on weight for *Raging Bull*, or Meryl Streep affecting a newly-researched accent for every film. Bogart was not versatile by these standards, nor even by those of his own time – not as versatile as James Stewart, say, or Cary Grant. His range of vocal and physical mannerisms was small, and he was rarely comfortable unless playing a part that he could base upon aspects of himself. So the question of personality soon becomes central to any assessment of his work.

After even a quick, nervous survey of the vast literature on this subject, however, you realize that you are standing on the edge of a minefield. Or, to shift the metaphor a little, you start to regard Bogart himself as a battle-ground on which various writers have fought their own battles for supremacy. Where is the real Bogart to be found, amidst the partisan biographies of his friends and admirers, the more sceptical essays of Louise Brooks and Kenneth Tynan, and the casually damning anecdotes of those who never got further than his prickly façade? Alistair Cooke knew him better than most, and was aware of the extent to which opinion was polarized: 'Some people

saw nothing but a moody drunk, a barfly given to random practical jokes and spasms of sadism, a cynic with more than a touch of paranoia leading to tasteless verbal assaults on anyone who conveyed a hint of pomp or authority or the lacier attributes of homosexuality. Others, who knew him well, found him gentle, gallant, modest, full of an indulgent or rueful humour, courteous with strangers, quietly and acutely sensitive to the plight of guests who were shy or being left out.'

It does not take long to realize that these contradictions also formed the basis of many of the characters he portrayed on screen. 'As I suspected,' says Captain Renault to the supposedly cynical Rick in *Casablanca*, 'you're a rank sentimentalist.' Rick provides the most extreme expression of a quality that informs all Bogart's most popular performances, one that it has been traditional to regard as combining toughness with an appealing vulnerability: the harder the shell, according to this theory, the more precious and fragile are the feelings it seeks to protect.

Bogart played variations on this theme in one film after another – some of them great, some of them worse than indifferent. This success depended very heavily on the quality of his collaborators. In *The Big Sleep* and *To Have and Have Not*, Howard Hawks quickly grasped the essence of the Bogart character and knew exactly how to exploit it, and yet everyone concerned with *Sirocco* seems to have thought

that you had only to take a world-weary and disillusioned anti-hero, plonk him in an exotic setting, engineer a last-minute shift from neutrality to idealism and – *voilà* – you'd got yourself another *Casablanca*.

The paradox here is that a character who has always been admired by audiences for his uncompromising individualism should have been brought into being by the most collaborative of all media. For this reason I think we can understand Bogart better if we regard the tension that his characters so often embody as lying not so much between toughness and vulnerability, as between power and powerlessness. Because we are all of us engaged in lifelong battles against authority, fought in the full knowledge that we live at the mercy of influences outside our control, we come to recognize in these brittle, formulaic melodramas – as Bogart struggles to assert himself against the weight of his romantic obsession in *Casablanca*, or against the entanglements of plot in *The Big Sleep* – echoes of our own predicament. On screen, Bogart can appear uniquely admirable because his genius seems to be for keeping a hold on situations even when the most hostile forces are crowding in upon him. And this without any action-man heroics, but by calling upon resources that are, in theory, available to all of us: quick reflexes, a cynic's familiarity with the world's ways and a line in sharp-edged, keep-your-distance humour which usually manages to leave his opponents

standing. But if these, too, were aspects of his own personality, where did he learn them?

An important point to remember about Bogart is that in an acting career that spanned thirty-four years, he spent more than twenty of them without any sort of control over the roles he was allowed to play. The condition of an actor under contract to a major studio has been compared by Louise Brooks – in all seriousness – to slavery. In the five years between his two 'breakthrough' films, *The Petrified Forest* and *High Sierra*, Bogart made twenty-nine movies, and although some of them were atrociously bad there was little to be gained from complaining, because the attitude of his bosses at Warner Brothers could best be summed up by one of the most characteristic lines from *The Maltese Falcon*: 'Take it and like it.' The fact that he ever did get to play the kind of parts he wanted – those that most closely resembled himself – is down to the same combination of luck, cunning and persistence that repeatedly got Sam Spade and Rick and Harry Morgan out of their tight corners. Expecting an actor to manifest anything approaching autonomy or individualism under the studio system was almost as far-fetched as asking Rick Leland, at the end of *Across the Pacific*, to turn the tables on the roomful of Japanese who are holding him captive. The remarkable thing, of course, is that Bogart did it, both times.

It was only in the movies, however, that he did it single-handed. The story of his success in real life is also the story of the people with whom he came into contact: the writers, directors and co-stars who wrote the speeches, fed him the lines, photographed the face and choreographed the movements that continue to hold cinema audiences in thrall. Some of these people had little insight into his abilities; others understood them better than he did himself. Some of them never got to know him well, and others became close friends. One of them, as we all know, even went so far as to marry him. So it would be a mistake, at the outset, to think that Bogart could ever have got to be Bogart without a bit of help.

This is not to belittle his achievement, merely to give proper weight to the randomness and chance element in a life that in some ways got luckier as he got older. Certainly to start with the breaks were few and far between, and in taking the measure of Bogart's career we have to begin with a lean and protracted apprenticeship – a part of the story that, while it is the shortest to describe, must have been one of the longest to live through.

1

BROADWAY'S LIKE THAT

the early plays & films

Humphrey Bogart's sixty-ninth feature film, *Sabrina* (1954), is interesting for a number of reasons: it provides a rare chance to see him playing comedy; we can sense tremors of the dislike he felt for his co-star, William Holden; it is a flawed but characteristic attempt to marry cynicism with sentiment on the part of its director, Billy Wilder. Above all, though, it provides a tantalizing glimpse of the sort of person Bogart might have become had he not drifted into the acting business. As Linus Larrabee, the loyal, upstanding son of a wealthy Long Island family, with a black Homburg, a pin-stripe suit and a top job in the family business, he represents everything that his own parents must have wanted for the eldest of their children.

Dr Belmont DeForest Bogart ran his medical practice from an office on the first floor of the family's large, handsome and fashionably situated house in New York. (There was also a country place on Canandaigua Lake, where Bogart first developed his love of sailing.) His mother, Maud Humphrey, was a freelance illustrator; Bogart's first taste of fame came early, when she drew a sketch of him playing in his carriage and sold it to Mellins Baby Food for use on their labels. His biographers assure us that he was born on Christmas Day 1899, although it has also been claimed that this was a myth dreamed up by Warner Brothers for publicity purposes, and that the real date on

The future gangster and tough guy.

his birth certificate was 23 January of that year. If this is the case, it was a fiction that he was happy to live out for the rest of his life, throwing elaborate 'birthday' parties every Christmas Eve and not letting even Lauren Bacall in on the secret. This would have been strange behaviour, to say the least, from a man who was always revered by his friends for his 'unqualified honesty'.

Dr Bogart's wish was that Humphrey should go to Yale, and to this end he was sent first to Trinity School and then to the Phillips Academy in Andover, Massachusetts. He arrived at Andover in September 1917 and was dismissed in May 1918, clearly having shown little interest in his studies. 'I can only hope that this will prove the turning-point in the boy's life,' the headmaster wrote, 'and that from now on he will develop that serious purpose which he appears to have lacked thus far.' After returning home to his parents Bogart waited only a week before enlisting with the Navy, although he was never to see any combat. President Wilson announced that the Armistice had been signed on 11 November and it was sixteen days after that Bogart reported aboard the USS *Leviathan*, a huge troop-carrier which had previously been Germany's largest passenger ship, and which was capable of doing the round trip from New York to Brest in an unprecedented twenty-six days. Bogart served on the *Leviathan* for less than three months, was then transferred to the USS

Santa Olivia, and received his honourable discharge in June 1919. He had seen next to nothing of the hardships of warfare and said later that 'the war had not touched me mentally'. Thirty-five years later, all the same, he was to claim that aspects of his portrayal of Captain Queeg in *The Caine Mutiny* were based on some of the officers he had encountered during his own military service.

Back at his parents' house, he dabbled unenthusiastically in a succession of casual jobs, the longest-lasting being his employment as a runner for S.W. Straus & Co., the Wall Street investment house. This was the firm that handled Dr Bogart's finances, but the family connection does not seem to have helped his son to shoot up the corporate ladder. He worked there for a year, though, and was then given his first break not by his parents' financial advisers but by their next-door neighbour, a producer called William A. Brady who ran the Playhouse Theatre on 48th Street. Bogart had grown up alongside Brady's children, Alice and Bill Jr, and it was Alice, now an up-and-coming actress, who suggested to her father that perhaps Bogart could be taken on as an office boy.

It is hard to believe that Brady could ever have been very friendly with the Bogarts, since his background was not at all similar. He has been described by Ethan Mordden in his book *The American Theatre* as 'a one-time prizefight manager who brought the savvy of the carny

Seaman Bogart en route *for the* USS Leviathan. *The year is 1918.*

On stage in Cradle Snatchers *with Mary Boland.*

barker with him when he deserted the ring for the stage'. According to this portrait Brady also 'muttered to himself throughout run-throughs and saw directing as the business of keeping the actors from falling off the edge of the stage'. He saw little potential in Bogart but was happy to let him have a try at most things, even at directing the final scenes of a film called *Life* for his independent production company, World Films. 'I did a fine job,' Bogart recalled. 'There were some beautiful shots of people walking along the street with me in the window making wild gestures. There was an automobile chase scene in which a car ran into itself. So Mr Brady stepped in and directed the rest of it himself.'

After this débâcle Bogart was taken on as company manager for a touring production, *The 'Ruined' Lady*, at a salary of fifty dollars a week. He understudied some of the actors and was rewarded by Alice Brady with a small part in her next play, *Drifting*, and he cannot have made too bad an impression because in the

autumn of 1922 he was promoted to second lead in a comedy called *Swifty*. The director, John Cromwell, has described how Bogart came to be chosen for the part: 'He used to hang around the Playhouse Theatre with young Bill Brady and another kid named "Bull" Durham; they sat in on rehearsals just from interest, and a situation came up with one of those comedies when a part is under-written and you can't get a good boy to do it so you compromise. That's what this was: some-body thought of Bogart, who at that time was the most responsible, the most charming . . . the best of the three kids. He was, of course, goggle-eyed to do it, and I think he said to me once: "Mr Cromwell, what do I do? Do I face out to the audience when I speak my lines, or do I talk to the characters?" I went through all these things with him, but the play was an awful flop.' More than twenty years later Cromwell was to direct Bogart again, in the film *Dead Reckoning* (another awful flop).

He was luckier with his next play, *Meet the Wife*, which starred Mary Boland and Clifton Webb and ran for thirty weeks. This was the start of a steady climb up the Broadway ladder, and for the next five years he was to alternate hits like this with the occasional disaster along the lines of *Baby Mine* (1927), which attempted to reintroduce Fatty Arbuckle to an unreceptive public but closed after a mere twelve performances. Among his biggest suc-cesses were *Cradle Snatchers*, which had the

With Shirley Booth in Hell's Bells
*(1925). His stage career was erratic
but at least one critic thought him 'as
young and handsome as Valentino
. . . as graceful as any of our best
actors'.*

longest run of the 1925-26 season, and Maxwell Anderson's *Saturday's Children*, in which he co-starred with Ruth Gordon, making her Broadway début. (In her autobiography she sardonically observed that the central moral issue of this play was whether she and Bogart could 'keep house on a hundred and seventy-four dollars a month and still not get uptight over who smoked the most Camels'.) It was also during this period that Bogart began his lifelong love affair with alcohol. There were 5,000 speakeasies in New York City and he was a regular at such haunts as the Hotsy Totsy, the Clamhouse and Tony's, a popular watering-hole for writers and actors where the patrons included Alexander Woollcott, Dorothy Parker and Mark Hellinger (still a journalist at this stage but later to produce six of Bogart's movies and to become a close personal friend). Several writers have insisted on Bogart's sexual puritanism, but like many actors he seems to have had quite a penchant for chorus girls, and once boasted that 'I had had enough women by the time I was twenty-seven to know what I was looking for in a wife'.

The strange thing about that remark is that Bogart never 'looked' for a wife as long as he lived; the pattern seems to have been that women set their sights on him and found – thanks to his old-fashioned idealism and a marked emotional insecurity – that he was not in the least bit difficult to push up the aisle. His first marriage, to Helen Menken, lasted only a

With Paul Kelly and Mary Philips in the wartime melodrama Nerves *(1924). Four years later Mary became his second wife.*

With his first wife, Helen Menken: it was to be his briefest marriage.

19

year and a half. Menken was a successful actress and a good friend of Alexander Woollcott – then the most influential critic on Broadway – so Bogart's friends persuaded him that to marry her would be a good career move. Naturally it was nothing of the sort, and the marriage rapidly fell apart under the influence of petty quarrels about housekeeping, long separations brought about by work commitments, and Bogart's already fiery temper (he once gave Menken two black eyes during a particularly bitter argument). In April 1928, only a few months after the divorce had come through, he married another actress, Mary Philips, whom he had first met backstage in 1923. He and Mary had acted together in an unsuccessful wartime melodrama called *Nerves* in 1924, and now went on to appear as husband and wife in a frothy comedy, *The Skyrocket*, which was panned by most critics and folded after a brief and poorly attended run. But the Bogart/Philips marriage, although it too was marked by long and difficult separations, was altogether more satisfactory, and even after he and Mary divorced in 1938 they remained on good terms. In marrying her, at any rate, Bogart had effectively renounced bachelorhood for the rest of his life: his second and third divorces would be followed by immediate remarriages, so that in each case he had to survive only a matter of days without the womanly protection he obviously craved.

It was at around this time that Bogart made his début on film. He appeared in at least two shorts, the first being a two-reeler for Paramount called *The Dancing Town*, featuring Helen Hayes. Two years later, in 1930, he was in *Broadway's Like That*, a ten-minute musical comedy for the Warner Brothers' Vitaphone Corporation, alongside Ruth Etting and Joan Blondell. Nothing is known about the circumstances in which he made these films; they quickly disappeared from public memory and no longer survive in complete versions. They seem, however, to have been made in New York between acting jobs, and cannot in any sense be seen as the beginning of Bogart's Hollywood career. The first decisive step in that direction came later the same year, when he was given a screen test at the suggestion of his brother-in-law and boyhood friend Stuart Rose, and was subsequently put under contract to Twentieth Century-Fox.

He arrived in Hollywood expecting to be given the lead in a film called *The Man Who Came Back*, but soon found that just about every other Broadway actor was in town on the same assumption. The part was eventually given to Charles Farrell, and Bogart was taken on as his voice coach at $750 a week. After that he got his first taste of the factory-like methods of studio production when he found himself working on two films at once: *A Devil with Women* and *Up the River*. The second of these was by far the more interesting, since it gave him the chance – although he can hardly have realized it at the time – to work with one of Hollywood's greatest directors, John Ford, and one of its greatest actors, Spencer Tracy.

With Mona Maris in A Devil with Women, *Bogart's first feature film.*

Up the River, *in which he starred with Spencer Tracy, marked the beginning of a lifelong friendship. It was also the first and last time they worked together.*

Bogart and Tracy had already met at a play-reading at William Brady's house a couple of years earlier, but this film marked the beginning of their long-lasting friendship. (It was Spencer Tracy who coined the nickname 'Bogie', which was to be Bogart's preferred designation for the rest of his life.) Originally planned as a hard-hitting melodrama about prison life, *Up the River* was saddled with a screenplay by Maurine Watkins that was, in Ford's opinion, 'just a bunch of junk'. With the help of comedian Bill Collier, Ford rewrote the script himself and found 'there was so much opportunity for humour in it that eventually it turned out to be a comedy . . . We did it in two weeks. It was Tracy's *and* Bogart's first picture – they were great – just went right in, natural . . .'

The plot has Tracy as a hard-bitten jailbird who unexpectedly reveals his finer feelings when he intervenes to save a prison romance between two naïve youngsters, played by Bogart and Claire Luce. Although *Up the River* is all but forgotten now, it is fascinating to think that three talents of this calibre should have got together so early in their careers; and Lindsay Anderson has found in the film 'some recognizable Ford touches of slapstick and sentiment; the handling is fast and loose and the comedy of bad men behaving like naughty boys is artlessly disarming'. The only other major director Bogart found himself working with during his first stint in Hollywood was

Raoul Walsh, for whom he made *Women of All Nations* in 1931; but his part was so small that he was cut out of some release prints altogether, and this seemed only too symptomatic of the half-heartedness with which Fox were promoting him. After making *A Holy Terror*, his sixth feature film, he gave up and returned to New York.

The next few years were bleak for Bogart. His sister Pat had fallen prey to manic depression following a gruelling twenty-seven-hour delivery; his father's practice was on the wane and the family had left their Riverside Drive home and moved into an apartment building. Good stage roles were hard to come by, and he found himself increasingly dependent on the income from his wife's flourishing career. In 1932 he went back to Hollywood for three films, *Love Affair*, *Big City Blues* and *Three on a Match*. In the last of these he tried out a new kind of part – away from the handsome juvenile roles with which he had been associated – and was cast as a gangster, but this still didn't help him to make any kind of an impact. So it was back to New York again, to a city that was beginning to feel the bite of the Depression, and where the leading playwrights were finding it less and less appropriate to produce the sort of scatty comedies in which Bogart – king of the 'Tennis, anyone?' role – had so far made his small mark on Broadway. Instead, with the worrying spectre of Hitlerism raising its head in Europe, writers like Maxwell Anderson and

Robert E. Sherwood were turning to a more socially-conscious theatre, one whose aim – in the words of Lawrence Langner, then head of the Theatre Guild – was 'to produce plays which would publicize the blessings of democracy to an audience skating on the thin ice of financial distress'.

Bogart's own financial distress was becoming acute. A keen and accomplished chess player, he managed to make some money by taking on the experts who could be challenged at display matches held in the windows of some of the larger department stores, but this was not enough to support a lifestyle that by now – especially after the repeal of prohibition – encompassed nightly drinking binges. And matters were made worse in September 1934 when Dr Bogart died, leaving his son with $10,000 in debts. (He also left him a ruby, diamond and sapphire ring which Bogart wore on his right hand from that day onwards: it can be seen in most of his films.) His career stalled, his family broken up, his marriage amicable but far from perfect, Bogart could be found most nights drinking himself into oblivion in Tony's bar on 52nd Street. Louise Brooks remembers going there at about one o'clock one morning and finding him 'alone, drinking steadily, with weary determination. His head drooped lower and lower. When I left, he had fallen into his exhausted sleep, with his head sunk in his arms on the table. "Poor Humphrey," I said to Tony. "He's finally licked."'

The chess enthusiast, seen here in later, less straitened circumstances.

2

DEAD END

Warner Brothers,
1935-41

In May 1934 Bogart was appearing in *Invitation to a Murder*, a distinctly run-of-the-mill mystery thriller starring Gale Sondergaard. It ran for only a month or so, but during that time it was seen by one Arthur Hopkins, a Broadway producer-director who seems – in this instance, at least – to have been more perceptive than most of his peers.

Hopkins was in the process of assembling a cast for a new, wordy, allegorical thriller called *The Petrified Forest*, by Robert E. Sherwood. Leslie Howard had been chosen for the leading part – an embittered intellectual, Alan Squier, who arrives at an Arizona roadhouse called the Black Mesa Filling Station and Bar-B-Q, only to be held hostage there by Duke Mantee, a killer on the run from the police. Sherwood was already a friend of Bogart's and, looking for a way to help him out of his current impasse, he tried to talk Hopkins into including Bogart in the cast. The part he had in mind was Boze Hertzlinger, an ex-football player – something typically lightweight, romantic and undemanding.

Hopkins, however, had a better idea. Everybody else thought he was crazy at the time, but he recognized that in his opening description of Duke Mantee, Sherwood had drawn a portrait that bore an uncanny resemblance to Bogart himself. 'He is well-built but stoop-shouldered,' it begins, 'with a vaguely thoughtful, saturnine face.' The description is close enough so far. 'He is about thirty-five' (Bogart was exactly this age when the play opened) 'and, if he hadn't elected to take up banditry, might have been a fine left-fielder. There is about him one quality of resemblance to ALAN SQUIER: he too is unmistakably condemned.'

Perhaps it was this final detail that clinched it as far as Hopkins was concerned. In his book *The Worlds of Robert E. Sherwood*, John Mason Brown paints a vivid picture of Bogart at this period, stressing 'his driven power, his anguished dark eyes, the puffs of pain beneath them, and the dangerous despair which lined his face . . . He felt suicidal and looked it, and was the object of his friends' concern.' It was therefore not because of his toughness or ruth-lessness that Bogart was chosen to play Mantee – after all, he had played gangsters in films before without making much impression – but because actor and character had something even more fundamental in common: they were both men at the end of their tether.

After a two-week try-out run in Boston, *The Petrified Forest* opened in New York's Broadhurst Theatre on 7 January 1935. Leslie Howard got the best of the reviews, but Bogart's unshaven, strangely charismatic villain was popular with audiences, and the play settled down for an extended run. It was soon bought for the screen by Warner Brothers, who intended to keep Howard in the leading role but to recast the rest of the film, with the

From the New York stage presentation of The Petrified Forest; *Bogart is on the far left, Leslie Howard on the far right.*

Archie Mayo directs Bogart, Bette Davis and Leslie Howard in a scene from The Petrified Forest.

Part of Bogart's luck was to have been given a visually dominant role in the film.

part of Duke Mantee falling into the capable hands of their resident gangster-in-chief, Edward G. Robinson.

But Robinson wasn't keen. Like the other actors (Cagney, Muni and Raft) who had shot to fame playing gunmen, he was getting tired of this sort of characterization. 'I didn't want to go along and keep doing gangster parts,' he said, some years later. 'I was then on contract to Warner Brothers and I kept insisting that I wanted to get a variety of roles and I wanted to get away from the gangster category.' And as it turned out, his reluctance saved the studio from a potentially difficult situation, because Howard had already promised Bogart that the film of *The Petrified Forest* would never be made unless he was allowed to play Duke Mantee. Howard stood by his word, the subject of Robinson was tactfully dropped, and Bogart remained for ever grateful – so much so that, eighteen years later, he and Bacall named their daughter Leslie, in honour of his loyal co-star.

So he and Mary moved back to Hollywood, initially taking up residence at The Garden of Allah on Sunset Boulevard, a set of bungalows grouped around a swimming-pool, which was then a fashionable stopping-off point for writers and actors. Bogart was signed to a $650-a-week contract (small beer indeed, even in those days), and shooting began on the screen version of his most significant stage hit to date.

The Petrified Forest is not a watchable film today, and the fault lies firmly with Sherwood's flat-footed original, which fails to bring its action into any kind of relationship with the ideas it so solemnly seeks to embody. Each of the characters, instead of being allowed to develop with something approaching human flexibility, is made to seem simplistically archetypal: Alan Squier represents the weak-mindedness of intellectuals, while Mantee is 'the last great apostle of rugged individualism' in the 'Petrified Forest of outmoded ideas'. Meanwhile the Black Mesa Bar-B-Q is held up as a microcosm of a decaying civilization. When he wasn't writing for the stage, Sher-

wood was also a speechwriter for President Roosevelt, and this shows up in a play that repeatedly gives voice to its liberalism by means of rhetoric rather than drama.

More often than not during this period, plays were rewritten for the screen with a healthy lack of reverence for the original material; but unfortunately *The Petrified Forest*, because it had been so successful on Broadway and because it was the work of an over-respected playwright, was handled with kid gloves and transferred on to film with all its creaking theatricality intact. perhaps a director like Hawks or Walsh could have given it a good

With Edward G. Robinson in
Bullets or Ballots.

shaking-up, cut out the verbiage and turned it into a decent gangster movie; but instead the task of directing it was entrusted to Archie Mayo, a competent Warner Brothers journey-man but one whose name is not writ large in the pantheon of Hollywood's great visual stylists.

As it happened, this was probably to Bogart's advantage. At this point he was still very much a stage actor, and he might not have made such an impact had he been thrown into a film in which more cinematic tech-niques were called for. And whereas Leslie Howard and Bette Davis (as Gabrielle, the daughter of the roadhouse manager) have very little to do when they aren't speaking except scramble around on the floor and look fright-ened, Bogart has all the iconography of the gangster movie to draw on, so that he is im-mediately the focus of any cinema audience's attention. As Richard Schickel put it in his essay on Bogart, 'It is perhaps too much to say you couldn't take your eyes off him, but cer-tainly there is little else worth looking at.'

Although there were a few freelance actors in Hollywood at the time, most actors went for the security of an exclusive contract, which meant that you had the choice of either appearing in whatever film the studio offered you, or being put on suspension. In the bitterly disillusioned words of Louise Brooks: 'I can state categorically that in Bogart's time there was no other occupation in the world that so

closely resembled enslavement as the career of a film star. He had self-determination only in this: he might or he might not sign a film con-tract. If he signed the contract, he became sub-ject to those who paid his salary and released his films. If he did not sign the contract, he was no film star.'

Much has been written about the stream of indifferent parts that Bogart was forced to accept during his next five years with Warners. The story goes that after making a stunning appearance in *The Petrified Forest*, he was shunted into interminable gangster roles which gave him no opportunity to stretch his abilities; and that his whole film career prior to the making of *High Sierra* in 1941 is a wilderness of dull, best-forgotten appearances. None of this is entirely true: he was not always cast in minor or supporting roles, and he actually appeared in a number of interesting, high-profile productions. As a relatively new and in-experienced film actor, in any case, he could hardly have expected to walk straight into star-ring parts for a major studio.

Bogart's initial lack of authority on screen can be gauged from his next film, *Bullets or Bal-lots*, which stars Edward G. Robinson. It is an almost first-rate gangster movie, in which Robinson plays Johnny Blake, a cop with underworld connections. At the start of the film he appears to be dismissed from the police force, although this is in fact merely a ploy to deceive the mob: feigning disenchantment

with the forces of law and order, Blake joins up with the gangsters and proceeds to destroy their system from within. Needless to say, there is one hood who is so hard-bitten and mistrustful that he sees through Blake from the start: this is 'Bugs' Fenner, played by Bogart.

There can be only one decent part in a film like this. Blake's double-sidedness, his easy affinity with both the law-breakers and the law-enforcers, may be largely symptomatic of the unease that the film studios were starting to feel about their alleged 'glorification' of gang-sters, but it also provides the actor with scope for a layered performance. Bogart, as it hap-pens, plays a very similar part – but in a mili-tary, wartime setting – in *Across the Pacific*, made a few years later, but this is not to say he could have pulled it off at an earlier stage. As it is, in *Bullets or Ballots* Robinson brings to the role a fullness and vitality that wipe everyone else off the screen. In one of the funniest and most effective scenes, he is alone in a room that he suspects has been bugged by the gang-sters; locating the microphone without diffi-culty, he fires his gun right alongside it – thereby nearly deafening Bogart, who is listen-ing in on headphones in the next room. Bogart rushes out into the corridor, his hands to his head, and runs straight into Robinson, who asks calmly, 'What's the matter – did you hurt your ears?' The nonchalance with which he carries this off makes us feel we are watching not just an experienced cop outmanoeuvring a callow gangster, but also a marvellously assured film actor showing a novice how things should be done.

Bullets or Ballots was released in June 1936. July brought another Bogart film, *Two Against the World*; August brought another, *China Clipper*, in which he plays an airline pilot who has to fly to China through terrible weather, at the behest of Pat O'Brien; and October

brought yet another, *Isle of Fury*, based on a Somerset Maugham novel, with Bogart playing a fugitive from the law hiding out in the South Seas. (This was the only film in which he ever got to wrestle with an octopus.)

Bogart's next really worthwhile movie, though, was released at the beginning of 1937. *Black Legion* was the latest in Warners' series of social-problem films, focusing on the activities of a secret racist society in a small American town. In its effort to peel away the wholesome veneer of American life and look at the core of nastiness underneath, it is not dissimilar to Costa Gavras's *Betrayed* (1989) – although *Black Legion* is arguably more economical and better presented, without the later film's pretentious romantic throwbacks to Hitchcock's *Notorious*. And this time Bogart had no reason to complain about the casting, because he was given the pivotal, starring role of Frank Taylor.

This was an audacious decision on somebody's part. Bogart had given no particular indication of range in his previous performances, yet here he was having to make an audience believe in the transition from mild-mannered, hard-working family man, through stages of vindictiveness, hatred and murder to a final scene of anguished repentance in the courtroom. He seems slightly ill at ease in the early scenes, which are meant to establish Taylor's peaceful domestic life (something that Bogart himself had seen very little of in the last twenty

A scene from Isle of Fury. *(Bogart never gave a good performance while wearing a moustache.)*

Publicity still for Black Legion.

years), but the film grows in tension and atmosphere from the moment when a crisis is provoked at work: a colleague of Taylor's called Dumbrowski – who is Jewish, although the Production Code would not allow this to be spelt out – is promoted over his head. Spurred on by a jingoistic radio broadcast, Taylor takes the advice of another of the factory workers and attends a secret meeting of the Black Legion, a supremacist clique which he subsequently joins.

Reviewing the film in July 1937, Graham Greene commended it for realizing that 'the real horror is not in the black robes and skull emblems, but in the knowledge that these hide the weak and commonplace faces you have met over the counter and minding the next machine. The horror is not in the climax when Taylor shoots his friend dead, but in the earlier moment before the glass when he poses romantically with his first gun; not in the floggings and burnings but in the immature question at the inaugural meeting, "If we join up don't we get a uniform or something?"'

The preachiness of *Black Legion* is perhaps hard to swallow for modern audiences (it ends with a long speech from the judge extolling Lincoln, the Founding Fathers and the Bill of Rights), but it has several powerful scenes and Bogart is alarmingly convincing as the politically fickle worker, his decency crumbling in the face of what he sees as a personal snub, backed up by effective propaganda. It attracted enormous media attention, and many newspapers not only gave it good reviews but even took up its arguments on their editorial pages. For Bogart, then, it was a considerable advance on *The Petrified Forest*, and he would

With Bette Davis in Marked Woman. *Mayo Methot, centre left, would shortly become the third Mrs Bogart.*

have been justified in feeling frustrated that it did not immediately lead on to better things.

Another film that he made around this time, however, did have far-reaching consequences. This was *Marked Woman*, Bette Davis's first movie for Warners after they had successfully sued her for attempting to work in England while still under exclusive contract to the studio. A bowdlerized version of the Lucky Luciano case, it concerns the tyrannical control exercised by a gangster (Eduardo Cianelli) over a circle of prostitutes – except that here they are portrayed as 'hostesses' in a swanky night-club. It was directed unimaginatively by Lloyd Bacon, another Warner Brothers die-hard, who had little affinity for material with this sort of female focus (curiously, it was Bacon who made more films with Bogart than any other director – John Huston and Michael Curtiz included). The main strength of *Marked Woman* lies in its script, co-written by Robert Rossen, who went on to direct many interesting films, including the Paul Newman poolroom classic *The Hustler*. It provided Bogart with another good role (again, not as a gangster) as David Graham, the crusading DA who finally smashes Cianelli's vice ring; and it also provided a small part for a curvy, hard-faced blonde called Mayo Methot, who played one of the hostesses – and was shortly to become the third Mrs Bogart.

If *Marked Woman* gave Bogart and Mayo the chance to develop their relationship,

20 August 1938: another ill-fated marriage. 'He cried at every one of his own weddings,' Lauren Bacall once recalled. 'And with good reason.'

Bogart posing, no doubt at the
studio's request, with polo, tennis,
golf and archery gear. He didn't
enjoy any of these sports.

With Mayo and friend.

opinions vary as to where they first met: some say in New York, others at the house of writer Eric Hatch, in Beverly Drive, Los Angeles. What is certain is that Bogart's second marriage was in a bad way by this stage, leaving him wide open to a little distraction. Mary Philips was essentially a stage actress, and she frequently left Hollywood for months at a time while appearing on Broadway. In her absence,

Bogart had started to cut a lonely and not particularly popular figure. His constant complaints about the business of film-making led Raoul Walsh to nickname him 'Bogie the Beefer'; his obstreperousness ranged from the witty and the impishly subversive (asked in a press release to list his 'hobbies' he offered 'Paints floral designs on teacups') to the kind of cantankerous and abusive behaviour that had alienated Bette Davis on the set of *The Petrified Forest*. James Cagney, with whom he remained on friendly but distant terms, once observed, 'Not many people liked him, and he knew it. He said, "I beat 'em to it . . . I don't like them first."'

It was in this context that Bogart, who seems to have been one of those men who can't function very well without female support, fell in love with Mayo. It was not a happy choice: she was prone to bouts of extreme jealousy, and she was – or would shortly become – an alcoholic. But she could also be loud and lively and fun, and at least (unlike Lauren Bacall) she was keen on sailing: Bogart decided to call their first yacht *Sluggy*, which was his pet name for her. She moved in with him while he was still married to Mary Philips, and their wedding took place in August 1938, only days after the divorce from Mary came through. They had a row at the wedding and spent their first night of married life staying with different friends, thus beginning a pattern that was to become legendary in Hollywood. The Bogarts'

Mayo and Bogie on board the Sluggy.

drinking sprees and loud, violent quarrels (Mayo once stabbed him with a kitchen knife) were forever making the tabloid headlines and got them banned from many of the more discerning clubs and restaurants.

'I believe in the institution of marriage,' said Bogart in an interview at around this time, and certainly he believed in giving it a try: no sooner did he run away from one woman than he was on the way to the altar with another. He must have regretted this particular coupling soon enough, anyway. Beneath all the press stories about the 'Battling Bogarts', and behind all Peter Lorre's cheerful anecdotes about how easy it was to provoke them into extremes of destructive and antisocial behaviour (sometimes smashing up whole hotel rooms), it is possible to discern a sadder and more serious picture – a picture of what Richard Schickel has called 'two alcoholics (she being by far the sicker of the two) locked in a punishing and dismal mutual dependency'.

As far as Bogart's film career was concerned, Mayo divided her time between railing at the studio heads for not giving him better parts and having fits of jealous panic whenever he looked as if he might be becoming too successful. *Kid Galahad*, although one of his better films from this period, derives its vigour from the interplay between Edward G. Robinson and Bette Davis rather than from Bogart's role as a one-dimensionally evil boxing manager. He does have one good moment, however,

His most memorable scene from Kid Galahad: *'Your pants are too long to be cute.'*

39

when he snarls at Wayne Morris, 'You think you're cute? Your pants are too long to be cute,' at which point he whips out a knife and slashes the aforementioned garments until they resemble a natty-looking pair of shorts. Next he co-starred with Pat O'Brien in *San Quentin*, in which he plays a convict who escapes but becomes ennobled through the love of his sister, and gives himself up only to die at the prison gate. (Another gem from the Lloyd Bacon production line.)

Bogart's growing popularity was watched with envy by the other studios, and he was now made the subject of one of those impersonal swap deals whereby top actors and actresses would be loaned out like so many studio props. He was lucky, all the same, because Samuel Goldwyn wanted him for a plum part in a big-budget movie, *Dead End*, to be directed by William Wyler. This was Goldwyn's answer to the Warners' social-problem films – indeed, with Bogart and Allen Jenkins in the cast it could almost be mistaken for a Warners production, except that the sets look more expensive and are better lit. Set in the slums of New York, *Dead End* focuses on a bunch of kids whose heroes are the gangsters of popular legend, and on the efforts of an idealistic architect (Joel McCrea) to redeem them. The action starts when a notorious criminal, Baby Face Martin, returns to the neighbourhood to pay a sentimental visit to his mother and his childhood sweetheart.

Baby Face Martin revisits his sweetheart (Claire Trevor) . . .

. . . and his mother (Marjorie Main). This is one of Bogart's finest early scenes.

Bogart is excellent as Baby Face Martin, and at thirty-eight he still looks just about youthful enough to justify the nickname. The scene with his mother (Marjorie Main) was one of the most demanding he had ever played, and it crackles with good lines ('I've killed men for looking at me like that'). Generally speaking, *Dead End*, unlike *The Petrified Forest*, was vigorously adapted for the screen, with Lillian Hellman improving on the dialogue of Sidney Kingsley's play. But certain scenes did have to be watered down to meet the requirements of the Production Code – the main casualty being Bogart's relationship with his girlfriend (Claire Trevor). In the play she contracts syphilis; in the film we just have the general sense that she has 'gone to the bad'.

The street kids were played by a group of young actors from the original Broadway production, who soon went on to achieve fame for themselves as the Dead End Kids and, later, as the Bowery Boys. Although only one of them, Huntz Hall, actually came from the lower Manhattan area where the story is set, they brought a raw, violent and untamed feeling to the screen which audiences at the time clearly found titillating. Their off-screen behaviour could be equally unruly, and Cagney was to claim that, while he had had no trouble keeping them in line on the set of *Angels with Dirty Faces*, they once, during the filming of *Dead End*, stripped Bogart of his trousers. 'When it came to fighting,' Cagney said, 'he was about

William Wyler directing Dead End – *by far the better of his two films with Bogart.*

as tough as Shirley Temple.'

Bogart's next movie was a satire on the film industry called *Stand-In*, which is bright and amusing enough, but didn't give his career the fillip it needed. Apparently the director, Tay Garnett, was accosted by Mayo Methot in a restaurant and asked why nobody ever thought of casting her husband as a romantic lead, and the part of Douglas Quintain in *Stand-In* was what he came up with. He later boasted that 'his role in *Stand-In* was Bogie's first sympathetic part and catapulted him straight into the arms of Ingrid Bergman, Katharine Hepburn and Lauren Bacall', which is an interesting reading of history, to say the least.

In fact the part of Quintain is sketchy and poorly written, and this is a shame because on paper it looks like a prototype of the characterizations with which Bogart was to make his name in the 1940s. When Atterbury Dodd (Leslie Howard), a stuffy Wall Street banker, arrives in Hollywood to sort out the finances of the beleaguered Colossal Studios, he finds that Quintain is the company's lone voice of integrity and incorruptibility. (Bogart must have enjoyed this part, because it corresponded very much with his own self-image.) He is a film producer, hopelessly in love with the studio's top star and heading towards alcoholism: 'You'll end up in a straitjacket,' somebody warns him. 'Why not?' he counters, 'You forget better that way.' Another leading question – 'Doesn't the fate of 3,000 people mean

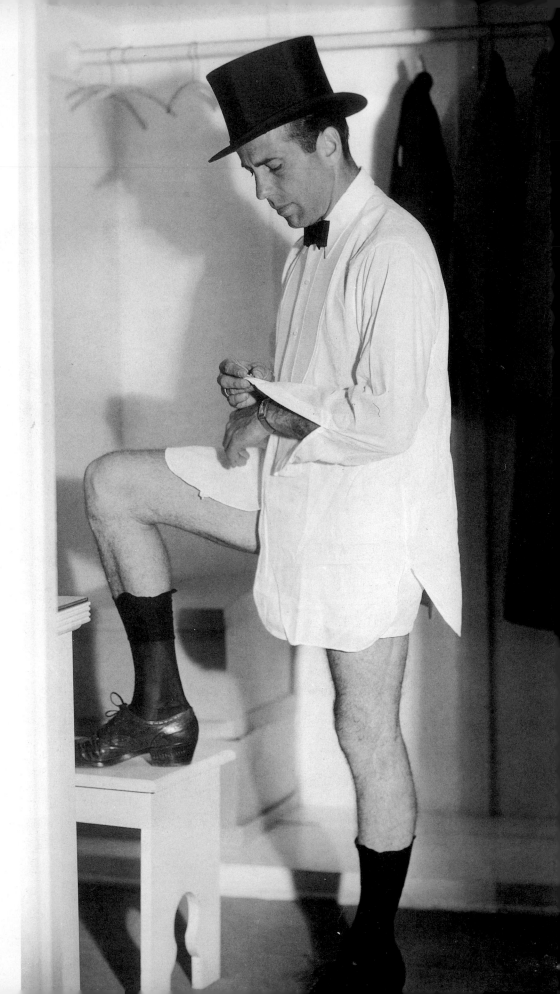

Dressing for the part of Douglas Quintain in Stand-In.

With Leslie Howard in Stand-In.

anything to you?' – elicits the even more typical Bogart retort 'Only the fate of one person means anything to me.' If these lines sound as though they might have come from his later, more fully-developed persona, the surrounding fluff and frivolity of *Stand-In* prevent them from having any resonance at this stage. However, it remains interesting as a premonition of the Bogart to come, as well as being fairly entertaining in its own right.

For the purposes of *Stand-In* he was on loan to producer Walter Wanger, and now Warners, seemingly impressed by the film's success, decided to try him out in a comedy of their own. *Swing Your Lady*, however, was a dismal fiasco, which Bogart forever afterwards referred to as his worst film. Historically it might have some importance, since it is the only surviving example of that little-known genre the hill-billy musical farce about the wrestling business. When you hear that its soundtrack included such showstoppers as 'Mountain Swingaroo' and 'Dig Me a Grave in Missouri', you might get an inkling of why the trend never took off.

After another failed romantic comedy, *Men Are Such Fools* (set in the advertising business and directed by Busby Berkeley), Bogart was back on the gangster treadmill: his next three assignments were all crime pictures, and of these only *The Amazing Doctor Clitterhouse* had anything new to offer. It provides a whimsical variation on the plot and casting of *Bullets*

or Ballots, with Edward G. Robinson again infiltrating a criminal gang, and Bogart again being the only member to have suspicions about him. The twist is that Robinson is in fact a scientist, conducting research into the physiological effects of criminal activity. Critics at the time had reservations about Robinson's suitability for such a cerebral role, although of course he carries it off with aplomb, while

As wrestling promoter Ed Hatch in Swing Your Lady. *It was an insultingly bad part for his return to Warner Brothers.*

Bogart does his best with the thankless part of 'Rocks' Diamond, described by the amazing doctor as 'a magnificent specimen of pure viciousness'. The screenplay was co-written by a relative newcomer called John Huston, shortly to become one of Bogart's most valued friends and colleagues, and it already shows signs of his wayward, rather cruel sensibility. (Robinson is delighted to hear that one of the hoods has a brother at Harvard, and makes the mistake of asking what he does there. Answer: 'He's preserved in alcohol – he's got two heads.')

Angels with Dirty Faces features Bogart's first appearance alongside James Cagney, and marks a significant moment in the history of the gangster movie because it shows the genre plunged deep into a crisis of conscience. 'The Hoodlum and the gangster is looked up to with the same respect as the successful businessman and the popular hero,' complains Pat O'Brien's Catholic priest; and who was to blame for this state of affairs if not film-makers in general and Warner Brothers in particular? Using the Dead End Kids again, the film explores conflicting moral influences on the young inhabitants of a poor tenement area of New York, although the issue becomes slightly ludicrous when the sure and certain path to redemption is represented by participation in the church basketball game, as opposed to the kids' more usual pastime of hanging around the local pool room. This time Cagney carries the film, as the

Confronting Cagney for the first time in Angels with Dirty Faces.

gangster Rocky Sullivan, the object of the kids' unhealthy adoration, while Bogart, as his corrupt and vindictive lawyer, has little to do. He does, however, have one fine scene of close-up facial gymnastics, as he listens to a radio broadcast about O'Brien's attempts to crack down on the gangsters: his lips go through every motion of anxiety, horror, outrage and contempt while chewing away edgily on a cigarette. The mechanics of screen acting were coming to him, slowly – although the discrepancy between his contribution and Cagney's, as far as the studio was conerned, can be judged from their respective fees: $8,800 (Bogart) compared to a cool $85,667 (Cagney).

They were paired again in *The Oklahoma Kid*, which was notable both for James Wong Howe's gleaming photography and for its general lightness of touch, as if everyone concerned knew that you could hardly put these two actors in a Western and expect people to take it seriously. Cagney had high hopes for this film at first: 'The picture was an idea of Ted Paramore's, who conceived of doing the story of the mountain men, particularly of their paragon, Kit Carson. We researched it and I came up with some things I wanted to do, pretty exciting things, I thought. Warners, without warning, pulled Paramore off the script and, without a word to me, changed directors. When I got the final script it had as much to do with actual history as the Kat-

zenjammer Kids. It had become typical horse opera, just another programmer.'

The plain and authentic clothing that Cagney had chosen for himself was replaced by 'the fanciest kind of cowboy costume', including a bizarre hat which, in Bogart's memorable phrase, made him look like a giant mushroom. Bogart himself was clad entirely in black and equipped with wavy hair, a side parting and the improbable name of Whip McCord. In the circumstances we can only be grateful that the two stars – and Cagney in particular – chose to coast through the film with tongue in cheek.

Hard on the heels of *The Oklahoma Kid* came *Dark Victory*, perhaps the most interest-

ing example in Bogart's career of casting against type. The fact that he was chosen to play the mild-mannered but romantic stablehand to Bette Davis's slowly expiring heiress seems to have been due, in part, to pressure from the screenwriter, Casey Robinson, who had been nurturing this project for more than three years. Robinson, at any rate, is another person who has claimed credit for revolutionizing Bogart's career, saying that it was his performance in *Dark Victory* that 'had gotten him out of gangster roles'. It is also true that Bogart's one big confrontational scene with Davis – without which his part would have been entirely negligible – was not only included at Robinson's insistence but actually

Whip McCord meets the Oklahoma Kid – no milestone in the history of the Western.

directed by him, since Edmund Goulding refused to shoot it. It is a taut and cleverly underwritten encounter, and while Davis conveys most of the emotional charge it is a relief to see Bogart playing a gentle and soft-spoken character for a change (his Irish accent is very creditable). This was the closest he had come, so far, to revealing anything of the private self that his closest friends were always describing, and we can only regret that the final sequence of the film was deleted, since it took the

characterization even further: after her death, Davis's horse, Challenger, was to be seen winning the Grand National, and Michael was supposed to lament, 'If only the little lady could have been here to see it.' 'Tears are streaming down his tough face' at this point, according to the published screenplay, but the scene was cut after preview audiences found it disappointingly anticlimactic, and so we have been robbed of a rare image of Bogart crying on film.

Opinions vary widely as to how successful Bogart was in *Dark Victory*. Bette Davis, with whom he habitually had bad working relations, was generous: 'I thought his performance was just perfect. We had some very difficult scenes to play . . . I thanked God for the help his performance gave me in playing mine.' Louise Brooks, on the other hand, writing in the 1960s, thought he was 'stricken with grotesque, amateur embarrassment', and this has become the received view. In any case, if it

Opposite and above: the much-disputed stable scene from Dark Victory, *in which Bogart was either 'just perfect' or 'grotesque' and 'amateur', according to taste.*

marked a step on the road to more demanding
and emotionally complex parts, his progress in
that direction soon received a hefty setback.
Pleasantly surprised by his performance in
Dark Victory, Warners now offered him the
lead opposite Bette Davis in her new picture,
The Old Maid. Executive producer Hal Wallis
announced this decision in a memo to the casting director, dated 22 February 1939, and it
seems to mark quite a shift in the studio's per-
ception of Bogart's potential. Sadly, he failed
to rise to the challenge. Exactly a month later
he was taken off the film – after only four days
of shooting. A studio report states that 'Messrs
WALLIS, BLANKE and GOULDING looked at the
scene with BOGART in the R.R. STATION and
decided to take him out of the picture', but
Charles Higham, in his biography of Bette
Davis, tells the story more dramatically: 'Humphrey Bogart was cast as the romantic hero,
and . . . he was so hopeless in a scene at a rail-
road station in which he left for the Civil War,
looking so thin and pathetic in his uniform and
so unromantic in his last wave goodbye, that
Warner demanded he be fired and Goulding
and Wallis were forced to tell him he was dismissed forthwith. he stalked off in a rage.'

And so it was back to gangsters again. Ever
sensitive to criticisms that they were glorifying
the criminal community, in *The Roaring Twenties* Warners found a new way of ducking the
charge, by treating the film as a period piece. It
begins with dates flashing across the screen

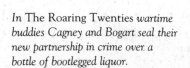

In The Roaring Twenties *wartime
buddies Cagney and Bogart seal their
new partnership in crime over a
bottle of bootlegged liquor.*

As the sinister Marshall Quesne in The Return of Doctor X. *The bunny's days are clearly numbered.*

until we are back in the year 1918, and the whole movie is bound together by a strident *March-of-Time*-style commentary. It represented a return to top form by director Raoul Walsh (although the early scenes were shot by Anatole Litvak, who made *The Amazing Doctor Clitterhouse*) and once again functioned primarily as a showcase for the dynamism of James Cagney. With its unusually long time-span (the action of the film is meant to stretch over more than ten years, even if none of the characters seems to age much), and its new stress on romantic entanglements, it marks the point at which the gangster movie starts to blur into the soap opera, with Cagney's Eddie Bartlett bearing a superficial resemblance to the character of Rick in *Casablanca*: like Rick, he has a piece of music that brings back memories of a faithless woman, except that here it is 'Come to Me My Melancholy Baby'. Bogart, needless to say, has nothing so interesting to occupy him – just the usual twitching, killing and general meanness – and we feel that he might be talking about acting rather than racketeering when he says to a colleague, 'Lefty, how do you like being a stooge?' When Lefty admits that he doesn't care, Bogart mutters ominously, 'Well I do. I think maybe I'll have to do something about it.'

For the time being, however, there was nothing Bogart *could* do about it. His career reached something of a nadir with *The Return of Doctor* X, a cheap and opportunistic sequel –

seven years late – to the classic Lionel Atwill movie. Here he plays a vampire, complete with fetching little round spectacles and a garish white streak in his hair. He later said that 'it was one of the pictures that made me march in to Jack Warner and ask for more money again . . . I was this doctor, brought back to life, and the only thing that nourished this poor bastard was blood. If it had been Jack Warner's blood maybe I wouldn't have minded as much.' Students of Bogart in unsuitable make-up could shortly compare this with his appearance in another Western, *Virginia City*, where he sports a pencil-thin moustache and the sort of sideburns that didn't come into fashion until the early 1970s.

It All Came True was more rewarding, but largely for reasons that had nothing to do with the film itself. Not that it isn't fun: Bogart plays Chips Maguire, a fugitive gangster who hides out in a boarding-house filled to the roof with dotty showbusiness types, and there is some lively if predictable comedy to be had from the clash of these two worlds. But more importantly, it was through this film that Bogart met the writer Louis Bromfield, upon whose novel *Better than Life* it was based and who was to become perhaps his closest friend. After writing a succession of novels, including the Pulitzer Prize-winning *Early Autumn* (1926), Bromfield had recently returned to his native Ohio, where he went on to experiment with scientific farming. He published several

Not looking quite at his best in a pose for Virginia City, *in which he was partnered with Errol Flynn.*

journals and diaries describing this experience and putting forward his (conservative) political views. It sounds an unlikely friendship, not least because Bromfield generally despised film people, and was once quoted as saying, 'The only good thing I can say about Hollywood is

Bogart lives there.' His friendship extended to Mayo, too, and in years to come he was to keep in touch with her – even to the extent of putting her up at his farm in Ohio – during her most difficult period, after Bogart had left her for Lauren Bacall.

Brother Orchid and *They Drive by Night* wrapped up this phase of Bogart's career. Neither was a bad film, but neither did anything to enhance his reputation – particularly as Warners continued to give him no higher than third billing. *Brother Orchid* found him

Lloyd Bacon, left, made more films with Bogart than any other director. Here Bogart and Robinson are running a scene from Bacon's Brother Orchid.

With Edward G. Robinson in
Brother Orchid.

*A measure of Bogart's status in
1940: the poster for* Brother Orchid
doesn't mention him at all . . .

. . . and he has to be content with fourth billing for They Drive by Night.

stuck with the most humourless role in a film where the sole point of interest is the joky idea of a notorious gangster (Edward G. Robinson) taking refuge in a monastery and succumbing to the charms of the devout life. Bogart holds his own in the first half of *They Drive by Night* as Paul Fabrini, one of a pair of truck-driving brothers, in scenes that were pacily handled by Raoul Walsh; but midway through the film he loses an arm in an accident and the focus shifts on to the sparring between George Raft and Ida Lupino. Bogart may well have resented the way he had to hand the movie over to them, but he would soon be facing up to Lupino on a more equal footing. And – ironically – it would be George Raft whom he had to thank for this and for some of the other chances that were to come his way in the next two, crucial, years.

3

THE BIG SHOT

1941-43

The release of *High Sierra* in January 1941, breathed life not only into the dying gangster movie but also into a screen career that was by now in serious need of resuscitation. Again Bogart is cast as a criminal – this time as a killer called Roy 'Mad Dog' Earle, who has been sprung from prison to assist with a big hotel robbery – but now the character has a more human, sentimental side. This is conveyed, heavy-handedly, by having him take pity on a family with a young crippled daughter: he pays for her to have an operation and is then heartbroken when she declines to marry him out of gratitude. History has therefore tended to regard the film as the first to give expression to a 'new', softer Bogart persona – although this is to forget the diversity of the parts he had played during his first few years at Warners. What really distinguished *High Sierra* was its fortuitous combination of talents – producer Mark Hellinger and director Raoul Walsh, with John Huston and W.R. Burnett writing the screenplay from the latter's novel – coupled with the fact that Bogart was for once given the leading role.

Originally George Raft was to have starred in the film. It seems incredible now that the monotonous, wooden-faced performances turned out by Raft throughout the thirties could have made him one of Hollywood's biggest box-office draws. When he signed to Warners in 1939, the studio presumably thought they had acquired a great asset in this man who (in the words of Jack Warner) 'once admitted that he could barely read, and never learned to write anything except a scrawled "Sincerely Yours" on fan pictures'. But the association soon ran into problems. The best-publicized was on the set of *Manpower*: Raft for no apparent reason started throwing punches at his peaceable co-star, Edward G. Robinson.

Warners had another, more long-term difficulty with Raft, however. If Bogart had a limited range, Raft had no range at all: he could play gangsters, and other thugs, and that was about it. (And he could only play them because they made up most of his circle of friends.) Yet he had an unwritten agreement with Jack Warner that he would not be required to play 'heavies' in Warner Brothers films. A letter that he wrote (or got someone to write on his behalf) to Warner on 17 october 1939 laments that he did not have specified in his contract 'the fact that I would not have to play heavies'. If there was one thing worse than playing 'heavies', in Raft's book, it was playing 'dirty heavies'. And if there was one thing worse than playing 'dirty heavies', it was playing 'parts that Humphrey Bogart should play'. Raft's petulant whining rises to a pitch as he reminds Warner 'you told me that I would never have to play a Humphrey Bogart part'. Since the studio could never think of any other kind of part to offer him, he spent most of his time at Warners on suspension for turning work down.

The original (above) *and re-release* (below) *posters for* High Sierra *show the extent to which Bogart's star would rise following the Oscar-winning* Casablanca.

As Roy 'Mad Dog' Earle.

Enjoying a lighter moment with 'Zero', one of his co-stars in High Sierra. Note Bogie's stacked heels.

A myth has been built up around the casting of Bogart in *High Sierra*, suggesting that it was one of those astonishing strokes of fate by which some men prove themselves to be ordained for greatness. It has been claimed, for instance, that he took the part only because of his theory that an actor should always be working; and when his agent rang to ask him whether he was prepared to do it, he is supposed to have replied, with wonderful nonchalance, 'Sure. Where the hell's the script and when do I start?'

The reality looks rather more complex. Hal Wallis, then executive producer at Warners, has said that Raft 'wouldn't act in *High Sierra* because the character died in the last reel. He was very superstitious.' But when W.R. Burnett was told of this theory, his reply was succinct: 'That's bullshit.' *His* version was that 'Bogie talked Raft out of it and got the part himself', which seems much more likely. Bogart knew the part was a good one and did everything he could to get it. After Raft, Warners offered it to Paul Muni, and when the news got around that he wasn't keen either, Bogart sent a personal message to Hal Wallis (dated 4 May 1940):

DEAR HAL. YOU TOLD ME ONCE TO LET YOU KNOW WHEN I FOUND A PART I WANTED. A FEW WEEKS AGO I LEFT A NOTE FOR YOU CONCERNING 'HIGH SIERRA'. I NEVER RECEIVED AN ANSWER SO I'M BRINGING IT UP AGAIN AS

With Ida Lupino, one of several female co-stars who found Bogart difficult to work with.

Signs of marital strain for Bogart and Mayo as they step out in public.

I UNDERSTAND THERE IS SOME DOUBT ABOUT MUNI DOING IT. REGARDS. HUMPHREY BOGART.

Whatever wiles he may have used to scare Raft away from the film (which was also, in some versions of the story, offered to Cagney, Robinson and John Garfield), Bogart took the part and did it more than justice, demonstrating again that he tended to give his best performances when playing characters with whom he could feel a strong personal affinity. Just as in *The Petrified Forest* he was able to identify with Duke Mantee's desperation rather than with his cruelty, so in this film he convinces as Earle not because the character is a ruthless killer, but because he is middle-aged and disillusioned. It seems particularly appropriate that Earle should make a last bid for rejuvenation by proposing marriage to a woman half his age: lucky for Bogart that when, four years later, he did the same thing himself, the results were a great deal happier.

This was the third and best of his films with Raoul Walsh, whose terse, unemphatic direction would sometimes provoke despairing memos from Hal Wallis ('Let's try to get some composition, and some moving shots, and some interesting stuff in the picture'), but here provided an expansive context in which Earle's characterization could develop. The most exciting scene in the film, it should be said, is the final, very long car chase against a back-

drop of grimly spectacular scenery – and this is a triumph for the director, not the actor. Bogart, by all accounts, was not easy to work with on the set of *High Sierra*. His marriage to Mayo was continuing on its noisy, violent, downward spiral, with both participants drinking more heavily than ever. Added to this was the fact that Bogart, having made no fewer than twenty-nine films in a little under five

years, was feeling somewhat jaded about the whole business. Walsh seems to have been good at taking the tantrums in his stride. He later recalled, 'When Bogart had one too many, he used to come and complain about his lines: "What a load of garbage, that script!" – "But you approved it," I answered – "I must have been drunk. You'll change that for me, won't you?" Then I changed a couple of lines

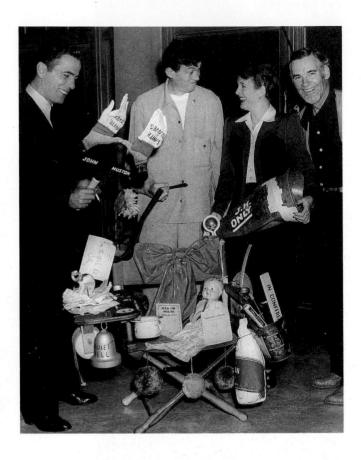

George Raft and Bogart getting to know each other in a scene from Invisible Stripes *(1939). There was no love lost between these two. Perhaps Bogie was right not to trust a man who kept his shoes on in the shower.*

Day one of shooting on The Maltese Falcon. *First-time director Huston is surrounded by Bogart, Mary Astor, his father Walter and an assortment of good-luck presents. (The director's chair came from William Wyler.)*

and he was happy and we could start working again.' But his co-star, Ida Lupino (who in fact took top billing), evidently had a rougher ride: after making this film, she made the studio promise that she would never have to work with Bogart again.

Success in *High Sierra* was still not quite enough to transform his career. He was now miscast as a carnival boss in *The Wagons Roll at Night*, a dull remake of *Kid Galahad* with the action transferred from the boxing ring to the circus ring. George Raft does not seem to have been offered this part – a good job, perhaps, because he was still in the business of turning down everything in sight, including the roles of Leach in *The Sea Wolf*, on the grounds that it was 'just a little better than a bit', and Sam Spade in *The Maltese Falcon*, on the grounds that it was 'not an important picture'. On the face of it this latter was a fair enough objection – the film was to be John Huston's first shot at directing – but it still didn't give Raft an adequate excuse for refusing the part. Instead he made use of the clause in his contract that said that he didn't have to appear in remakes; *The Maltese Falcon* was technically a remake, since Dashiell Hammett's novel had been filmed – unfaithfully – twice before.

Bogart himself was on suspension at this point, having just turned down a Western called *Bad Men of Missouri* ('Are you kidding . . .' was his only response when he was sent the script). It was obviously a bad part, but also

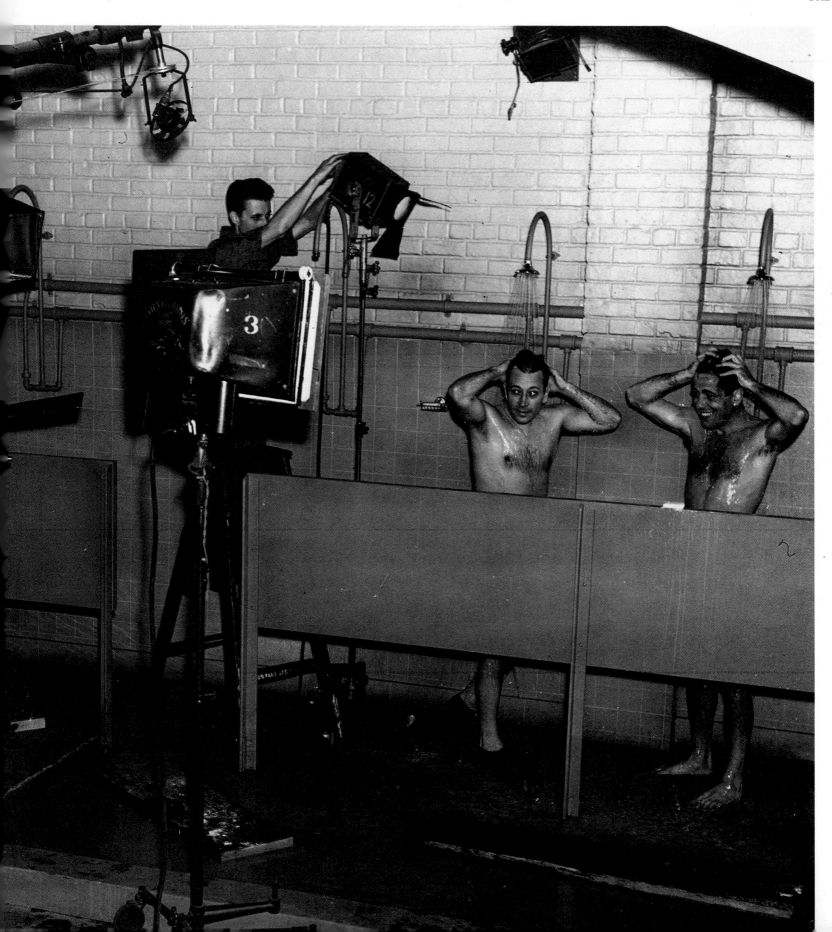

With Mary Astor in The Maltese Falcon.

he was in a huff after being dropped from the cast of an altogether more prestigious project, *Manpower*, when the star of the film had declared his refusal to work with him. That star, needless to say, was George Raft – who can thus take double credit for getting Bogart the lead in *The Maltese Falcon*, by both turning it down himself and indirectly ensuring that his rival wasn't working at the time when Warners were frantically scouting around for a replacement. Pleasant though it would be to believe otherwise, it seems after all that film history is made less by destiny than by the coincidences of studio politics and the random collision of volatile egos.

One person who responded with undisguised delight to the casting of Bogart was John Huston himself. 'I thanked God,' he said. 'It was a blessing.' A great deal was at stake for him and he had strong ideas about how the film should be approached. Neither of the previous versions had been successful because, in his opinion, the adapters had been 'assholes, idiots' with 'no understanding . . . of what Dashiell Hammett had done'. His overriding consideration was fidelity to the written material – not only the plot, but even the style and the grammar of the original novel. 'I implicitly accepted Hammett's writing . . . I attempted to transpose his highly individual style into camera terms with sharp photography, geographically exact camera movements, and striking but not shocking set-ups.' This made

for a crisp and clear presentation of Hammett's potentially bewildering narrative about a laconic private detective (Bogart), a *femme fatale* who also happens to be a pathological liar (Mary Astor) and a golden falcon from the fourteenth century, 'crusted from head to foot with the finest jewels'. In contrast to *The Big Sleep* there are no loose ends here, although after an initial preview Jack Warner was sufficiently confused to suggest reshooting the opening scenes in order to 'tell the audience what the hell it is all about', and, according to Mary Astor, 'John Huston often had to call time out to clear up matters. All of us had read the Dashiell Hammet book and studied the script, but it got so that when the "now just a minute" look came on to somebody's face, it became a joke to say, "When did Brigid shoot Thursby? On Friday!"' At the last minute it was decided that a line of dialogue was needed to cover the moment when Sidney Greenstreet finds that the falcon is a fake, and you don't have to listen too hard to realize how crudely such additions were made: the voice is that of another actor, and little effort was made to match Greenstreet's distinctive timbre.

The luckiest thing about *The Maltese Falcon*, as far as John Huston was concerned, was that the studio's expectations were so low. In the first place he had saved them money by choosing to adapt a property that they already owned; and since nobody regarded it as much

'The Huston troupe': John Huston,
Peter Lorre, Mary Astor and Bogart
– all 'very fast company in the wit
department'.

Bogart, Lorre, Astor and Greenstreet on the point of discovering, at the end of a long and meticulously rehearsed scene, that the Falcon is a fake after all.

Bogart as Sam Spade.

more than a B-movie, he was under no pressure to fill the cast with big names. Bogart therefore found himself at the head of a decidedly motley crew: Astor, a freelance actress, seemed incapable of keeping her career on course for more than a year or two at a time, and was still trying to recover from the publication, in 1936, of scandalous extracts from her personal diaries; Sidney Greenstreet, who plays Bogart's adversary Kaspar Gutman, was a sixty-two-year-old British actor who had never made a film in his life (shortly before shooting his first scene he came to Astor and said, 'Mary dear, hold my hand, tell me I won't make an ass of meself!'); and Peter Lorre never did fit into the Hollywood mainstream, having fled his native Hungary and worked in many European cities as a travelling actor before achieving his biggest successes playing psychopathic killers in films by Fritz Lang (*M*) and Hitchcock (*The Secret Agent*).

The atmosphere on the set of *The Maltese Falcon*, then, was scarcely that of a typical Warner Brothers production, and suddenly Bogart felt that he was in his element. It was unusual for the members of a cast to get on so well that they wanted to socialize with each other, but the nucleus of the *Falcon* team – Bogart, Huston, Lorre and Astor – found that shooting was proceeding well ahead of schedule and started to take increasingly long lunches and dinners together at the Lakeside Golf Club across the highway from the

Top billing at last.

Warners studio. Here, said Astor, 'People from other companies would eye us suspiciously because we weren't wolfing down sandwiches in a hurry to get back to work.' She also recalled, 'The combination of Huston, Bogart and Lorre was very fast company in the wit department; there was a kind of abrasive, high-powered, kidding-on-the-level thing that went on, and you joined in at your own risk.'

The film's associate producer, Henry Blanke, who referred to them as 'the Huston troupe', would occasionally petition Hal Wallis to authorize unusual filming procedures. For the long final scene in Spade's apartment, for instance, a whole day was set aside simply for rehearsal, when normally it was unheard of for

the cost-conscious Warners to let a day go by without at least *something* ending up in the can. They scrutinized Huston's rushes daily, and – incredible though this may now seem – their main worry was that the film was going to be too slow. Huston responded firmly but diplomatically to their suggestions, although his patience must have been sorely tested by some of Wallis's less helpful remarks (for example, 'The scene in the apartment with Bogart, Astor and Peter Lorre is very good. I don't think it is too slow. It could just stand a little speeding up . . .').

Apart from anything else, the studio was worried, as usual, that Bogart himself would not be able to carry the film. 'I think my

Huston's father Walter graced the movie with a brief cameo as Captain Jacobi. Huston got a perfectly satisfactory first take and then made him do the scene again and again. It was his idea of a joke.

criticism is principally with Bogart,' wrote Wallis, 'who has adopted a leisurely, suave form of delivery. I don't think we can stand this all through a picture, as it is going to have a tendency to drag down the scenes and slow them up too much. Bogart must have his usual brisk, staccato manner and delivery, and if he doesn't have it, I'm afraid we are going to be in trouble . . . We must get away from this method of delivering the dialogue, particularly on the part of Bogart.' In the opinion of Louise Brooks, this problem was never resolved: 'In *The Maltese Falcon* his part was uncomplicated, but too much dialogue betrayed the fact that his miserable theatrical training had left him permanently afraid of words. In short speeches, he cleverly masked his fear with his tricks of mouth and voice, but when, in this film, he was allotted part of the burden of exposition, his eyes glazed over and invisible comic-strip balloons circled his dialogue.'

This is an uncharitable view of a performance that, for the first time, found Bogart looking genuinely relaxed and comfortable in front of the cameras. The reason seems to lie in the affinity he clearly felt for Sam Spade's teasing moral ambiguity. He had played characters with more than one side to them before, but this was not the simplistic double-sidedness of Joe Kennedy in *San Quentin*, with his sudden and last-minute moral transformation, nor even the crude dichotomy that animated Roy 'Mad Dog' Earle, the notorious killer with a

soft spot for lame girls and furry animals. The character of Spade is taut with ambiguity from the word go, and his energy derives from any number of intriguing tensions: loyalty to his dead partner while he has also been having an affair with that partner's wife; allegiance to the law while he is also constantly being threatened with imprisonment; a pose of self-sufficiency and independence while he is also as quick as anyone to fall into the arms of Brigid O'Shaughnessy; and so on. Beneath all this was a deeper tension, fundamental to the classic Bogart persona, between an ironic fatalism (his belief that life does not count for much) and an indisputable courage (his will to preserve it at all costs, nevertheless). 'You won't get into any trouble, will you?' Astor asks him at one point, and Bogart's reply – 'I don't mind a reasonable amount of trouble' – tempers its expression of bravery with a more desperate undertone implying that heroics are all very well, but the really important thing in life is to avoid being bored.

Did Bogart actually display these qualities in real life? Probably not. It seems more likely that his Sam Spade is convincing for the more general reason that he felt very much at ease playing a character who gives so little of himself away. Standing over the body of Spade's partner, Miles Archer, a police officer seems desperate to provoke Spade into expressing some kind of emotion: 'I guess everybody has their good points,' he prompts, but Spade's

answer is defiantly non-committal: 'I guess so.' What the audience senses here is not absence of feeling, but a distant suggestion of feelings so complex that Spade sees no point in bringing them to the surface. As an actor, Bogart seemed never happier than when he was able to give this impression, and he was quick to acknowledge *The Maltese Falcon* as having provided him with an unrivalled opportunity: 'I had a lot going for me in that one. First, there was Huston. He made the Dashiell Hammett novel into something you don't come across too often. It was practically a masterpiece. I don't have many things I'm proud of . . . but that's one.'

The next two films gave him nothing like the same scope: he played a gangster in both *All Through the Night* and *The Big Shot*, although the gangster movie – much to Bogart's relief, no doubt – was by now definitely on the wane. In the Nazis, Hollywood had found a new set of baddies to vilify, and instead of bringing life to one-dimensional heavy roles, Bogart was now faced with the (equally unrewarding) task of bringing life to one-dimensional patriot roles. Flushed with the success of *The Maltese Falcon*, Warners re-assembled Huston, Astor, Greenstreet and Bogart and put them to work on *Across the Pacific*, a propaganda piece which serves only to demonstrate how important Dashiell Hammett's watertight plotting and dialogue were to the success of the earlier picture. In this case,

As Duke Berne in The Big Shot *– a disappointing return to the gangster format.*

With Greenstreet and Astor in
Across the Pacific; *the cast is the
same but the magic has gone.*

anyway, the screenwriter (Richard Macaulay) had the difficult job of ensuring that his story kept pace with real events: it was originally going to be about a Japanese plan to bomb Pearl Harbor, and when this did in fact happen the whole thing had to be rewritten and ended up being a Japanese plan to bomb the Panama Canal. There is much pleasure to be gained from watching these performers swapping banter again, but Huston's apparent readiness to regard this as the film's *raison d'être* is an early indication of the complacency that sometimes marked his career, reaching its apogee in *Beat the Devil* twelve years later.

Across the Pacific is also a frustrating film to watch because it almost but doesn't quite know how to use Bogart properly. For a while we are allowed to believe that his character, Richard Leland, really has left the army in disgrace. 'I haven't got a history,' he says defensively, when questioned about his past, and – like Harry Morgan in *To Have and Have Not* – he declares his willingness to be hired out to whichever side pays the most, including the Japanese. In order to make it the kind of part Bogart would have relished playing, all that would have needed to happen next was for Leland's latent patriotism and decency to crawl out from their protective shell, transforming him into a man of action and ideals. But sadly, his cynical amorality has been a pose all along, he is actually an undercover agent, and the gun-toting finale fails to thrill because as soon as he starts saving the world single-handed Bogart becomes a bargain-basement James Bond, lacking all human credibility. Besides, John Huston had by now left to join the war effort, and the closing scenes, directed by Vincent Sherman, have a tired and

John Huston leaves for war with the final scenes of Across the Pacific *uncompleted.*

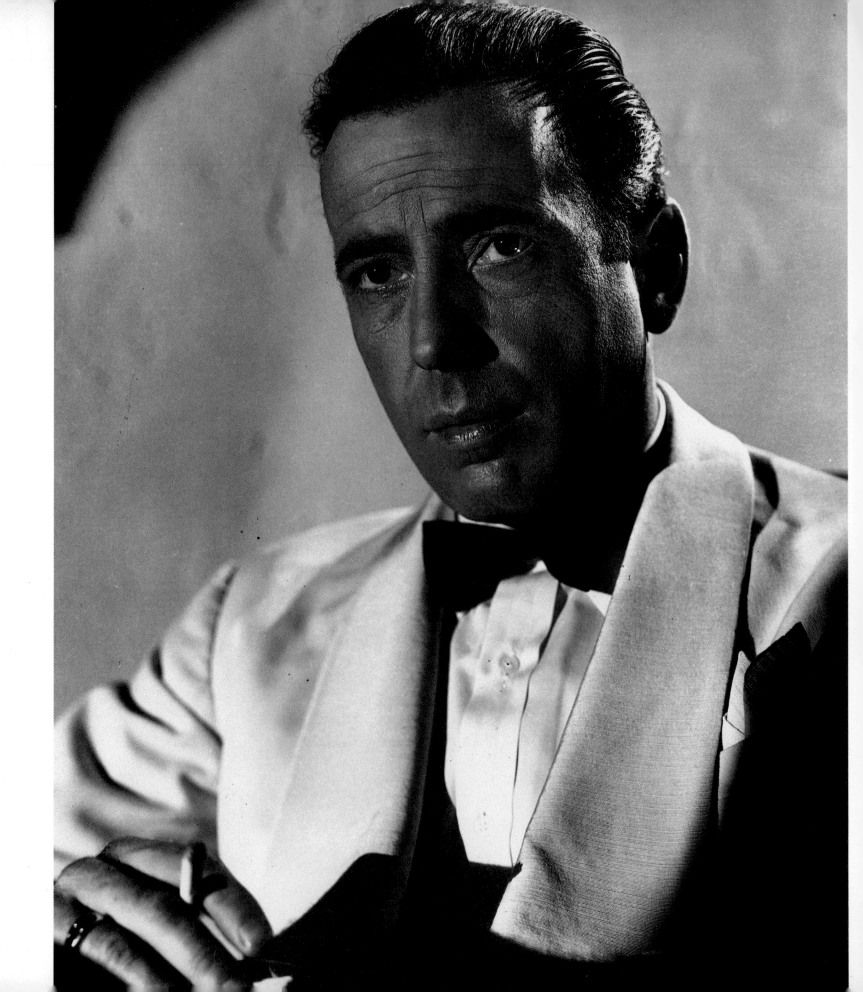

perfunctory feel to them.

There is one unintentionally poignant moment in *Across the Pacific*, when Bogart says to Mary Astor, 'I look old, but that's because I've worried a lot.' His face had indeed aged considerably since his marriage to Mayo. It had been round about that time that he had played the character called Baby Face Martin in *Dead End*, but no one seeing the battle-scarred features he was about to present in *Casablanca* would have thought of using the nickname Baby Face Rick – and yet only five years had passed between these films. Louise Brooks, whose famous essay on Bogart is full of unexpected perspectives, believed that 'Except for Leslie Howard, no one contributed so much to Humphrey's success as his third wife, Mayo Methot'. According to Brooks, there were powerful feelings of envy, hatred and violence within him which 'she brought to a boil, blowing the lid off all his inhibitions for ever'. Even Brooks, however, was horrified by what she saw of the Bogarts at the 21 Club in 1943: 'They sat at a table in the far corner of the room as if they wanted to be alone, yet they neither spoke nor looked at each other till their drinks were brought to the table . . . I was shocked to see how dreadfully Humphrey's face had aged. The effects of the war he had waged against his inertia – work and whiskey without sleep and food – were visible at last.'

To locate the source of the pain and world-weariness that Bogart projects so memorably in

Casablanca, then, we need only consider the wretched state of his own marriage while he was making it. Ironically, the film itself made things worse, because Mayo was convinced that he had fallen in love with Ingrid Bergman. She needn't have worried – the two stars were never close. Bergman once remarked rather wistfully in this connection, 'I kissed him, but I never really knew him.' But if Mayo could confuse the on-screen romance between Rick and Ilsa with an off-screen affair between Humphrey and Ingrid, it only goes to show the extent to which Bogart encouraged his fictional characterizations to become entangled with his real, everyday self. And when he continued to show nothing of himself to Bergman, ungenerously denying her the glimpses of contact with which she might have been able to build a rapport, she fell back, revealingly, on his film performances as the only source of insight into his character: 'He was polite naturally, but I always felt there was a distance; he was behind a wall. I was intimidated by him. *The Maltese Falcon* was playing in Hollywood at the time and I used to go and see it quite often during the shooting of *Casablanca*, because I felt I got to know him a little better through that picture.'

In truth Bogart was bad-tempered and worried during the making of this movie, and not only for reasons connected with his marriage. Like everybody else involved, he was convinced the film was going to be an abject

Portrait taken in 1944 by Philippe Halsman, revealing how Bogart had aged in the previous few years.

failure. *Casablanca* was conceived in a spirit of confusion and uncertainty which was never entirely shaken off, and there is now so much argument·over who actually wrote the screenplay that the matter is certain to remain unresolved – except in so far as one can say that anybody who happened to be hanging around Warner Brothers during the summer of 1942 probably had something to do with it.

If his own story is to be believed, it was Casey Robinson (screenwriter of *Dark Victory*) who first drew Hal Wallis's attention to an unproduced play by Murray Burnett and Joan Alison called *Everybody Comes to Rick's*, which the studio subsequently bought for $20,000. Having received various unpromising reports on it from his story analysts, Wallis had it marked down as a B-picture, probably to star Ronald Reagan and Ann Sheridan, until one day a producer called Pan Brennan astonished him by saying that he thought it was Humphrey Bogart, out of all Warners' leading men, who held the most appeal for women. The thought had apparently never occurred to Wallis, but he now began to think of the newly renamed *Casablanca* as a potential Bogart vehicle.

Initially the screenplay was assigned to two writers, Wally Kline and Aeneas MacKenzie, neither of whom was particularly enamoured with the property. After less than a month they were replaced by the Epstein twins, Julius and Philip, who also made slow progress:

The men behind the movies. Left to right: Hal Wallis, D.C. Dobie, Jack Warner and J. Walton Brown. Wallis did more than anyone to bring Casablanca *to the screen, but it was Warner who got up to collect the Oscar.*

Michael Curtiz directs Bergman and Bogart in the famous last scene.

Rains, Henreid, Bergman and Bogart. They didn't always look this happy during the making of Casablanca.

Julius, at one point, was entrusted with the difficult task of visiting David O. Selznick and convincing him that his latest protégée, Ingrid Bergman, should be loaned to Warner Brothers in order to star in a film that at this stage didn't even have a story. Then America entered the war and the Epsteins, in response to a summons from Frank Capra who needed help on his series of propaganda films, *Why We Fight*, put their patriotism above their commitment to the *Casablanca* scenario and left for Washington, leaving behind little in the way of usable material.

With only a few weeks to go before shooting was to begin, Wallis brought in a younger writer, Howard Koch, to knock the screenplay into shape. Meanwhile the casting problems multiplied. Word was getting around that a prestigious film was in preparation and none other than George Raft started angling for the lead. Jack Warner seemed on the point of agreeing to the idea when Wallis weighed in and stuck up for Bogart (at last): 'Bogart is ideal for it, and it is being written for him, and I think we should forget Raft for this property. Incidentally, he hasn't done a picture here since I was a little boy, and I don't think he should be able to put his fingers on just what he wants to do when he wants to do it.' For the part of Sam, Rick's pianist and loyal sidekick, Wallis considered two female performers, Hazel Scott and Lena Horne. In the end he settled on Dooley Wilson, although this did

The most famous toast in cinema history: 'Here's looking at you, kid.'

Rick and Ilsa enjoying their brief romantic idyll in Paris. These flashback scenes appear to have been written largely by Casey Robinson.

present problems during filming, as Wilson couldn't play the piano to save his life and found it difficult to mime convincingly to the prerecorded soundtrack.

Shooting on *Casablanca* started on 25 May 1942, and by this time the Epsteins had written two-thirds of the script, Howard Koch was working on his own version, and Casey Robinson had read the composite screenplay and written a detailed report on it, making many important structural suggestions that were certainly incorporated into the finished film. (He was eventually paid $6,000 for his three and a half weeks' uncredited work on *Casablanca*. Koch got $4,200 and the Epsteins $15,000 apiece.) But nobody yet knew exactly how the story was going to end, and the tone of the film seemed to be pulling in three different directions according to the different temperaments of the writers: romantic (Robinson), political (Koch) and comic/satirical (the Epsteins). The cast and crew were bewildered from the very beginning. 'Every day we were shooting off the cuff,' Ingrid Bergman recalled. 'Every day they were handing out the dialogue and we were trying to make some sense of it. No one knew where the picture was going and no one knew how it was going to end, which didn't help any of us with our characterizations. And all the time I wanted to know who I was supposed to be in love with, Paul Henreid or Humphrey Bogart?

'"We don't know yet – just play it well . . . in between."

'I didn't dare to look at Humphrey Bogart with love because then I had to look at Paul Henreid with something that was not love.'

Every day Hal Wallis would visit the set and argue with the director, Michael Curtiz. Curtiz had long arguments with Bogart, and valuable shooting hours would be wasted as they sat around trying to decide how on earth they were going to play scenes that had been delivered only that same morning. At lunchtimes Bogart would retreat into his dressing room with Howard Koch to discuss the finer points of Rick's characterization. Koch would scream and yell at Curtiz for bringing in other writers to tamper with the logic of 'his' script, to which Curtiz's famous retort was 'Don't worry what's logical. I make it go so fast no one notices.' One victim of this directorial strategy was Claude Rains, who was once asked to do nine takes of a scene that involved nothing more complex than walking through the door into Rick's café. Exasperated, he asked Curtiz what exactly he was doing wrong, and was told, 'I want you should come in faster.' After consulting briefly with a props man, Rains said that he was ready to do the scene again; the cameras started rolling, the door was thrown open, and he entered on a bicycle.

Such moments of light relief were rare, and did little to dispel the prevailing mood of panic. Frantic revisions were still being carried

Dooley Wilson plays it again.

Claude Rains gives the order to 'round up the usual suspects'.

out to the script, and everybody was throwing in suggestions (it was Bogart's own idea that Rick should be seen playing chess at the beginning of the film, for instance). The final scene continued to pose the biggest problem: how could Rick be made to shoot Major Strasser without immediately being thrown into prison, and thereby ending the film on a downbeat? It was the Epsteins' idea that Renault should turn a blind eye to the killing, by repeating his earlier line 'Round up the usual suspects': it came to them simultaneously (so the story goes) as they were driving down Sunset Boulevard late one night. And it was Hal Wallis's idea that the last line of the film should be 'Louis, I think this is the beginning of a beautiful friendship' – a line that Bogart had to dub on to the soundtrack more than three weeks after shooting had closed down. It is surprising how often the most memorable closing lines are the product of last-minute improvisation: another example is 'It's the stuff that dreams are made of', which rounds off *The Maltese Falcon*. This wasn't in the screenplay either, but was the inspired suggestion of Bogart himself.

If the question of who wrote the *Casablanca* screenplay can never be settled conclusively, perhaps authorship of the film should be ascribed to Hal Wallis, who not only exercised general creative control but also kept up a stream of specific ideas and suggestions on everything from the story to the way the set was lit. Every Sunday Michael Curtiz and the writers would gather at Wallis's ranch to discuss the progress of the script, and he insisted on numerous changes which included, mysteriously, the removal of a 'gargling' scene (and quite what *that* would have involved we shall probably never know). He also oversaw the assembly of the music soundtrack: it was Wallis who suggested that 'As Time Goes By' should run as a motif throughout the film (Max Steiner hated the idea and the tune), and who thought up the telling moment in the final scene when the music suddenly stops, the aeroplane propellers jerk into action and then the orchestra starts up again with renewed urgency. At the Oscar ceremony at which *Casablanca* won the award for best picture, Wallis was about to get up on stage to receive it when Jack Warner sprang ahead of him and collected it himself. Wallis was so amazed and mortified at this downgrading of his own contribution that he resigned from Warner Brothers immediately, and he spent the rest of his career as an independent producer.

The internal politics behind the making of *Casablanca* have been discussed here at such length because they remind us that its success depends on a blend of quite disparate elements – romantic, comic and political – held in unusually fine balance. If *Casablanca* is complex, that may be because nobody could decide quite what to do with it. The romantic scenes are without doubt the most unevenly written, and they contain the screenplay's handful of

Bogart hobbles his way through a
scene in Conflict with an equally
miscast Sidney Greenstreet. 'Why
don't you burn this script up and
forget about it?' he asked Jack
Warner.

truly dreadful lines: 'A franc for your thoughts'; 'Was that cannon fire, or is it my heart pounding?'; 'Oh Victor, please don't go to the underground meeting tonight'. Poor Ingrid got lumbered with all of these, as if it weren't bad enough not knowing which of the leading men she was meant to be making eyes at. But Bogart gave a miraculously authoritative performance, and it is his presence that holds the film together. The script's greatest danger lay in the temptation it offered for the central character to lapse into self-pity, but Bogart keeps this possibility at arm's length, and instead transforms Rick's implausible broken-heartedness into a peculiarly American quality – one that Michael Wood, in his book *America in the Movies*, has described as 'a dream of freedom which appears in many places and many forms, which lies somewhere at the back of several varieties of isolationism and behind whatever we mean by individualism, which converts selfishness from something of a vice into something of a virtue, and which confers a peculiar, gleaming prestige on loneliness'. With one film Bogart had made this quality his own. It has been impossible, ever since, to associate it with any other actor.

As for *Casablanca* itself, Umberto Eco has tactfully remarked that it 'represents a very modest aesthetic achievement'. As he also points out, however, the film's extraordinary richness lies in the very desperation with which it anthologizes every genre at once –

from the adventure story to the *film noir*, from the propaganda movie to the weepie. Of course, if this had been done carelessly, the result would have been the most unwatchable sort of self-parody. It is important that the film is superbly shot, lit, scored, edited, acted and directed, so that watching the finished product is like seeing all the best scenes from your favourite films, strung together into some kind of magically seamless whole. In Eco's words, '*Casablanca* became a cult movie because it is not *one* movie. It is "movies".'

If *Casablanca*'s status as a work of art can be described as 'very modest', Bogart's next two films, *Action in the North Atlantic* and *Sahara*, do not even register on the Richter scale of aesthetic achievement. Both are absolutely routine propaganda pictures, *Sahara* being marginally the more watchable of the two by virtue of Rudolph Maté's desert photography. Bogart was on loan to Columbia for this film, and then back at his own studio he had a run-in with Jack Warner over a movie called *Conflict*, in which he was supposed to play a man who murders his wife so that he can marry her sister (Alexis Smith). It took Warner numerous telephone calls and letters to get him to do this one, and the published transcript of one of these calls does not make very edifying reading. 'Nothing you can say will convince me it is a good picture, or is in good shape, or for me,' Bogart complained. 'I consider you a personal friend of mine and do not

Suppressed violence often lies at the heart of Bogart's performances, and in this curious moment from Passage to Marseille *he suddenly goes ape and starts gunning down the enemy.*

think you will do all the things you say you will.' Warner replied, 'In my opinion, from a professional standpoint, this picture now called *Conflict* will be one of the important pictures, because it is so different from anything that you or we have done . . . I have heard the same talk from twenty people who talk just like you are doing, and I know one of them is now trying to get a job as just an extra.' This seems an unusually unconvincing threat to brandish at the man who had just starred in

the hugely successful *Casablanca*.

It is true that Bogart was miscast in *Conflict* (although he wasn't the only one: Sidney Greenstreet tries, and fails, to get to grips with the part of the shrewd psychoanalyst, Mark Hamilton). He scowls his way through the film, hobbling around on a walking-stick, and his one moment of heroism – when he renounces Alexis Smith and gamely wishes his rival suitor good luck – is patently half-hearted, the palest shadow of Rick's rekindled

nobility. All the same, it is an atmospheric, engaging film from the heady days when Hollywood was just beginning to discover Freud, who would no doubt have been surprised to find his theories of sexuality reduced to the moral that 'love rather than money is the root of all evil'. All the clichés of the psychological movie are here – including that perennial favourite, the close-up shot of water spiralling away down a plughole to indicate mental turmoil (followed by echoing voice-overs and spooky faces drifting across the screen). 'Funny things happen inside people's heads, don't they?' Bogart muses, and this half-truth was to provide much source material for film-makers over the next few years – most notably in Hitchcock's *Spellbound*, which is both the most accomplished and the silliest example of the genre. Meanwhile Warners took one look at *Conflict* and shelved it: it was finally released in 1945.

Bogart concluded a busy working year with *Passage to Marseille*, the first of Warners' attempts to cash in on the success of *Casablanca*, for which they assembled many of the same cast – Bogart, Greenstreet, Lorre and Rains – and teamed them with the same director, Michael Curtiz. The plot, however, was carelessly chosen. (It took the intelligence of Howard Hawks to grasp the essence of the character of Rick and to build a new, improved vehicle around it, in *To Have and Have Not*.) In *Passage to Marseille* Bogart was miscast as a French journalist, Matrac, whose crusading anti-fascist activities have made him so hated by the establishment that he is framed on a murder charge and sent to Devil's Island. He manages to escape, along with four other convicts (one pauses at this point to wonder why Bogart is the only one without a trace of a French accent), and makes his way to England, only to be shot down while flying on a bombing mission for the Free French. It is never easy to believe in Bogart as an outspoken

Matrac the crusading journalist phones through another of his controversial stories in one of the many flashback scenes from Passage to Marseille.

man of ideals, which is so much the reverse of what he appears to have been in real life. (Quite the most unconvincing aspect of *Casablanca*, for example, is its suggestion that Rick used to run guns in the Spanish Civil War before being swept off his feet by Ingrid Bergman.) *Passage to Marseille* founders on this basic implausibility, a simple misreading of the boundaries that had already been clearly staked out by the Bogart persona. It remains interesting for its unusual narrative structure – flashbacks within flashbacks within flashbacks – which was later put to better use in a complex RKO melodrama called *The Locket* (1946).

On the set of *Passage to Marseille* Bogart was

Bogie and Mayo making a radio broadcast.

visited one day by Howard Hawks, who wanted him to meet the girl he was going to star with in his next film. Lauren Bacall gives a matter-of-fact account of this meeting in her autobiography, *By Myself*: 'There was no clap of thunder, no lightning bolt, just a simple how-do-you-do . . . Nothing of import was said – we didn't stay long – but he seemed a friendly man.' Bogart, perhaps, had more important things on his mind, such as how he was going to survive a trip he was due to make with Mayo to North Africa, where they were supposed to be entertaining the troops. Departing in December 1943, they were abroad for a little less than three months, at first in Africa and then in Italy. Bogart did speeches from his most famous films, starting off with an extract from *The Petrified Forest*; Mayo would sing songs, with accordion accompaniment, taking requests from the audience; and offstage they engaged in just about the most violent combat anyone at the front had ever seen. Bogart is said to have bashed down the door once when she locked him out of their hotel room, and had to apologize to a high-ranking officer the next morning for causing such a disturbance. Their marriage was clearly in a desperate state, but since these were the sort of scenes that had already been a matter of public knowledge for years, the only real puzzle – and one that raises more questions about Bogart than it does about Mayo – is why it had been allowed to last anything like as long as it did.

With Bruce Cabot in Casablanca on the couple's tempestuous morale-boosting tour to North Africa.

4

TO HAVE
AND HAVE NOT

the fourth marriage
& the first amendment

The popular image of Bogart is that of a fierce individualist with strong personal convictions and unshakable values, who refused to give in to the phoniness of Hollywood and remained untouched by the vanity that afflicts lesser movie stars, leading them to confuse their ordinary little selves with the heroic personalities they portray on the screen. And yet there was surely never a marriage that had so much grounding in the cinema, and so little in real life, as that between Bogart and Lauren Bacall. Like many happily married couples they were brought together by a matchmaker: in this case it was the director Howard Hawks. But he had envisaged their partnership purely in cinematic terms, and was surprised and apprehensive when he saw a romance that he and his scriptwriters had cooked up on celluloid suddenly about to spill over into real life. Years after giving Bacall her big break opposite Bogart in *To Have and Have Not*, he was to offer this curious verdict on the people whom everyone liked to regard as Hollywood's least phoney couple: 'The funny thing is that Bogie fell-in love with the character she played, so she had to keep playing it the rest of her life.'

Some critics have praised Hawks for his feminism, although he distanced himself from such claims and his films show little understanding of any other than a masculine sensibility. He believed in writing strong parts for women, but his idea of a strong woman was one who behaved like a man. This in itself, of course, would have been preferable to the insipid parts with which many actresses had to make do during the thirties and forties (and beyond), and one can imagine that for Hawks, the dissatisfaction of a film like *Casablanca* would lie in the role it assigned to Ingrid Bergman, as the passive bargaining-counter between Rick and Victor Laszlo. He began to imagine what it would be like if a director tried to match the Bogart character with an equally strong female presence.

A female counterpart to the Bogart persona emerged by chance after Hawks's wife, Slim, had drawn his attention to a picture of a model on the front cover of a recent *Harper's Bazaar*, and Hawks instructed his secretary to find out something about her background and acting experience. Obviously the wrong message was delivered, because the model, Betty Joan Perske, promptly arrived in Hollywood in the summer of 1943 expecting to meet Hawks and to be screen-tested. 'All of a sudden this kid appeared in a gabardine skirt and a sweater. She was only nineteen. And, well, she talked in a little high nasal voice. But she was so eager, she wanted to work and everything, that I couldn't send her home; I had to give her some kind of a chance.' So Hawks gave her a screen test, took her out to lunch, told her she should learn to speak in a lower register (which she did by reading aloud endlessly to herself in a parked car) and eventually put her under personal contract to himself. He also decided to call her Lauren, which she detested, although she was happy enough to adopt her mother's maiden name, Bacal, to which she now added an extra 'l'.

There was a combination of frankness and youthful determination in Bacall that Hawks found himself admiring, and one day he put a proposition to the screenwirter Jules Furthman: 'Do you suppose we could make a girl who is insolent, as insolent as Bogart, who insults people, who grins when she does it, and people like it?' This was the genesis of the character of Marie in *To Have and Have Not*. Hawks had bought the screen rights to Hemingway's novel because Hemingway had bet him that he wouldn't be able to make a film out of it: his solution was to jettison nine-tenths of the story and to concentrate on the relationship between Harry Morgan (Bogart) and Marie (Bacall). In the novel the couple are married and in their forties, but Hawks, considering this an unpromising situation, decided to turn the film into a speculation about how they might have met. Out went the book's social comment (making the title, with its reference to society's 'haves' and 'have nots', all but meaningless) and out went the Latin American setting, since a 'good neighbour policy' was in effect and the Office of Inter-American Affairs would not have granted an export licence to a film that depicted insurrection and smuggling taking

place in Cuba. The action was relocated to the Caribbean island of Martinique; Harry Morgan became a rugged individualist caught up in the struggle between the Vichy government and the Free French; and suddenly it looked as though everybody had another *Casablanca* on their hands.

As with *Casablanca*, the screenplay of *To Have and Have Not* was written only a day or two ahead of shooting, but since this was Hawks's preferred method of working nobody seemed especially worried. Bacall recalls that 'Each morning when we got to the set, he, Bogie and I and whoever else might be in the scene, and the script girl, would sit in a circle in canvas chairs with our names on them and read the scene. Almost unfailingly Howard would bring in additional dialogue for the scenes of sex and innuendo between Bogie and me. After we'd gone over the words several times . . . we'd go through the scene on the set to see how it felt. Howard said, "Move around – see where it feels most comfortable." Only after all that had been worked out did he call Sid Hickox and talk about camera set-ups.' William Faulkner, one of the co-writers, has expressed his approval of this method, saying that the best screenwriting was always done by 'the actors and the writer throwing the script away and inventing the scene in actual rehearsal just before the camera turned'. In this way it soon became obvious to everyone that the real interest of the film lay in the relationship between Bogart and Bacall: Hawks became less and less interested in the other aspects, and came to regard the entire plot as 'just an excuse for some scenes'.

Although it has affinities with *Casablanca* thematically, then, *To Have and Have Not* is light-years away in terms of atmosphere and mood. In place of Curtiz's fluid, restless direction, full of flourishes and virtuoso gestures, we

Howard Hawks, far right, discussing a typical last-minute change to the script of The Big Sleep *with John Ridgely. Bogie and Bacall seem more interested in each other.*

have an objective, non-committal camera which follows most of the action in medium shot, allowing the performers to develop their characterizations at a comfortable pace. Hawks was quite capable of pulling off the occasional action scene (witness the electrifying moment when Morgan shoots Captain Renard through the drawer of his desk), but by and large the tempo of the film is leisurely, almost unbelievably so in the first sequence aboard Morgan's boat, which is concerned less with setting the plot in motion than with establishing an ambience – male, breezy, outdoor, companionable – that is quite distinctive. Bogart had never looked more at home than in this setting; apart from anything else, it was the first film in which he had been able to demonstrate how good he looked when handling a boat.

'Bogie was one of the best actors I've ever worked with,' Hawks said. 'He certainly could do anything that you asked him to, and he also took criticism without a murmur.' He considered Bogart to be 'really underrated as an actor . . . Without his help I couldn't have done what I did with Bacall. The average leading man would have gotten sick and tired of the rehearsal and the fussing around. Not many actors would sit around and wait while a girl steals a scene. But he fell in love with the girl and the girl with him, and that made it easy.'

This unexpected turn of events first became

apparent, according to Bacall, about three weeks into the shooting of the picture. Immediately it presented problems, because Bogart was still very much married to Mayo, who was as watchful and as jealous as ever. A few weeks earlier, when he was congratulating Bacall on her screen test (which consisted of the famous 'If you want me, just whistle' scene), his prescient comment had been 'We'll have a lot of fun together', but for a while it seemed as if fun was the last thing on their

agenda: they would drive their cars to secluded residential streets and sit holding hands and talking, or write each other long, ardent, frustrated letters. And when shooting on *To Have and Have Not* was over, they had no further excuse for being together. Fortunately fate was quick to step in, in the kindly guise of Howard Hawks and the Warners executives, who were so pleased with the on-screen chemistry between the two stars that they decided to waste no time before pairing them again. In October

1944 they began filming *The Big Sleep*.

With this film Hawks did for *The Maltese Falcon* what he had just done for *Casablanca* with *To Have and Have Not*: that is, to take a similar plot and milieu but to harden the edges, make the pacing less rigorous, give the whole film an improvisatory feel and above all pit the Bogart character against a woman who was equally tough, insolent and sharp-witted (although Mary Astor already had a march on Ingrid Bergman in that respect). For this

purpose Hawks hired a new writer, Leigh Brackett, and was immediately in for a surprise: 'Leigh, I thought, was a man's name, and in walked this fresh-looking girl who wrote like a man.' He paired her off with William Faulkner, who, according to Hawks, 'didn't know anything about screenwriting. I put the two together; they did the whole script in eight days. And they said they didn't want to change things because the stuff was so good; there was no sense in making it logical. So we didn't.'

The cheerful disregard for logic flaunted in *The Big Sleep* is in fact one of its principal charms. Whole scenes would be written and shot simply because Hawks thought they might be fun, or, in the case of the bookstore scene with Dorothy Malone, 'because the girl was so damn good-looking'. For the previous scene Bogart turned up the brim of his hat and donned horn-rimmed glasses, and he brings off an effeminate characterization that is eerily different from his usual persona; throughout the shoot he improvised other minor details, such as the habit of fondling his earlobe while deep in thought, which was one of his real-life mannerisms. And although none of them has achieved the mythic status conferred by worshippers on 'Here's looking at you, kid' or the apocryphal 'Play it again, Sam', *The Big Sleep* is the film that contains all the best Bogart lines: 'Take it easy – I don't slap so good around this time of the evening'; 'Those are harsh words to throw at a man, especially when he's walking out of your bedroom'; 'She tried to sit on my lap while I was standing up'; 'Get up, angel – you look like a Pekinese.'

All the same, the making of *The Big Sleep* was a difficult time for everyone. Bogart had pretty much kept away from Bacall after finishing *To Have and Have Not*, but now they resumed their affair with a vengeance. Mayo knew all about it, and was busy going in and out of hospital: her drinking was even heavier now that she realized the marriage was on its way out. Bogart kept leaving home, checking into hotels and then going back again; he was drinking more than ever, too. A memo from Eric Stacey, unit manager on *The Big Sleep*, gives a taste of how serious things had become, and also shows the kind of mordant humour with which Bogart responded to the situation: The Hawks Co., while waiting for Mr Bogart this morning about 9.15 . . ., received a phone call for Mr Hawks from Mrs Bogart saying that Bogart had shown up at the house at 8.30 this morning very drunk.

I went out to the house with Bob Vreeland, talked to Mrs Bogart relative the situation, having previously contacted Sam Jaffe (Mr Bogart's agent), asking him to please come along. According to Mrs Bogart, Bogie was in a very bad condition and sleeping by the time we arrived – approximately 10.00 o'clock . . .

Mr Bogart himself appeared and the atmosphere became extremely strained and

The Big Sleep.

I felt that my presence there would serve no useful purpose since Bogart himself kept asking, 'Are we holding a wake?' . . .

I really do not feel that Bogart's condition can be straightened out overnight since he has been drinking for approximately three weeks and it is not only the liquor, but also the mental turmoil regarding his domestic life that is entering into this situation . . .

The studio production manager T.C. Wright recorded similar problems:

Dec. 20th – EXT. of HIDEOUT (Stage 19) – Thirty-minute delay, from 1.20 to 1.50 p.m. – conference. It was necessary for Mr Hawks to speak with Mr Bogart for a half-hour and straighten him out relative the 'Bacall' situation, which is affecting their performances in the picture.

At the same time Hawks and his wife were making other, more oblique attempts to straighten out 'the Bacall situation' – by desperately trying to fix her up with somebody else. They even laid on a dinner party for four, the fourth being none other than Clark Gable. 'He *was* dazzling to look at,' Bacall later conceded, 'but he stirred me not a bit. I tried to flirt a little, tried to be attracted to him – but it didn't work.' The upshot was that nobody was hugely satisfied with *The Big Sleep* when shooting was completed in January 1945, thirty-four days behind its forty-two-day schedule. The film had to wait eighteen months for its commercial release (although a version of it was shown to American servicemen abroad towards the end of the war) and meanwhile, in November, it was decided that some further scenes were required to bolster the Bogart/Bacall relationship which had, after all, been the main reason for doing it in the first place. Hawks, Bogart and Bacall knocked together the scene in a café where Marlowe and Vivian have an outrageously suggestive conversation about horse-racing ('Speaking of horses, I like to play them myself; but I like to see them work out a little first. See if they're front runners or come from behind'). Few people who see *The Big Sleep* today realize that this scene was shot almost a year after the rest of the film, and that in the meantime a small change had taken place in the relationship between the two performers – namely, that they had got married.

During this period, Louis Bromfield kept a diary of his life in Ohio, which he published in 1946 under the title *Malabar Farm*. The entry for 14 May – 6 June (1945) contains the following evasive passage: 'There has been a long stream of visitors of all kinds – farmers, industrialists, government officials, foreigners and friends. None of the bedrooms has been empty since March.' What he omits to mention – except that presumably it comes under the category of 'friends' – is that on 21 May Malabar Farm played host to the wedding of Humphrey Bogart and Lauren Bacall. Mayo had spent six weeks in Reno so that Bogart

The original poster gives Bacall equal billing and shows the extent to which they had already established themselves as a team.

Malabar Farm, 21 May 1945. Left to right: Louis Bromfield, Bogart, Mary Bromfield, Bacall's mother Natalie, Bacall, George Hawkins and Judge Shettler, who performed the ceremony.

Cutting the cake, with best man (and best friend) Bromfield looking on.

Bogart pays a visit to the set of Confidential Agent, *and uses it as an excuse to take on Charles Boyer at his favourite game, observed by former chess champion Herman Steiner. Bacall, it seems, is none too thrilled.*

could get a quickie divorce; he settled a large sum of money on her, and also gave her ownership of one of the two Safeway stores that he had bought as an investment. And now, for the second time, he found himself marrying one woman within days of divorcing another. The ceremony was squeezed in during the middle of his work on *The Two Mrs Carrolls* and a few days before Bacall had to start on her next film, *Confidential Agent*. Bromfield (who was best man) did his best to keep the press at

bay, although it was almost arranged for a *Life* photographer to accompany them on the train to Ohio. Bogart's comment on that was 'Great. Maybe he'd like to photograph us fucking.' Both he and Bacall wept copiously during the wedding ceremony. He had been nervous for days beforehand, and while the generally accepted view is of a whirlwind romance in which the partners were drawn to each other by an irresistible mutual attraction, it is worth pondering a remark that Bogart let slip to pro-

ducer Mark Hellinger: describing Bacall as a 'tigress', he said, 'I have the feeling of a mouse that's going to be torn apart by a rabbit.'

The marriage, in any case, was to prove his most lasting and stable, and having finally got his personal life into some sort of order Bogart now set about putting his career on an equally secure footing. He negotiated an unprecedented new contract with Jack Warner which stipulated that he had to make only one film a year for $200,000. He could also do one film a year away from the studio, could turn down two out of three stories submitted to him and could refuse to work with any director except the five specified in the contract: John Huston, William Wyler, John Ford, Billy Wilder and Edward Dmytryk. A curious list, in retrospect, especially in view of the fact that Howard Hawks doesn't appear on it.

The Big Sleep had none the less been released in August 1946 to general acclaim, and it managed to repair some of the damage done to Bacall's reputation by her dire performance in *Confidential Agent*, which Jack Warner in his wisdom had decided to put out first. At this point Bacall was still being promoted by Warners as 'the Look', while over at Paramount, where he was now working as an independent producer, Hal Wallis was trying to build up a rival attraction in the shape of Lizabeth Scott. (For this purpose he had decided that she should be known as 'the Threat'.) When Bogart and Scott found themselves on loan to Columbia at the same time, studio boss Harry Cohn must have thought he had a powerful combination on his hands, and he decided to pair them off in a picture.

Bogart was given free rein in his choice of director, and skimmed disparagingly down the proffered list of names until he came to one that struck a chord: John Cromwell – the same John Cromwell who had given him his first break in the play *Swifty*, when he was still hanging around Bill Brady's theatre in the

Signing the breakthrough contract, with his business manager Morgan Maree, his agents Sam Jaffe and Mary Baker, and, of course, Bacall.

On the Dead Reckoning *set with John Cromwell and Lizabeth Scott.*

early 1920s. He opted to work with him again, according to Cromwell, 'out of curiosity', but there was one problem: 'We had no story. They had the usual pile of stuff they always had handy to see whom they could pass it off on to . . . I finally got this one, a noxious sort of thing, but I felt perhaps we could make something of it.'

The 'noxious sort of thing' in question was *Dead Reckoning*, which turned out – unintentionally, it seems – to be almost a parody of the private-eye genre in general and *The Maltese Falcon* in particular. Like Sam Spade, Rip Murdock (Bogart) is trying to avenge the death of his partner; in this instance they were formerly paratroopers together. One's doubts about the film begin with the opening scene, in which Bogart is seen confessing the whole story to the priest they both knew from their parachuting days – 'the Jumping Padre', no less ('always the first out of the plane'). This confessional framework provides the excuse for a drawling voice-over commentary by Bogart, full of sub-Chandlerisms: 'Johnny's service record came to me like a photograph against the eyelids'; 'Stalled again – like a jeep on synthetic gas'. As a narrative device, it is borrowed shamelessly from *Double Indemnity*, and in lieu of that film's repeated references to the smell of honeysuckle, Bogart harps on the smell of jasmine in the hair of his supposedly alluring co-star. Sadly, Bogart and Scott generate nothing like the friction of Fred MacMurray and Barbara Stanwyck in *Double Indemnity*, let alone the Bogart/Bacall chemistry of the two Hawks films. Although statuesque and good to look at, Scott is hampered, in her big musical number, 'Either It's Love or It Isn't', by an unsuitably dubbed singing voice, and as an actress she was never lucky enough to be taken under the wing of a brilliant Svengali-like director, which had been the main factor in setting Bacall on the road to success.

Bogart was so devoted to his new wife that he made little effort either to look interested in Scott on screen, or to treat her with particular courtesy during the shooting. Like certain other actresses (Bette Davis and Ida Lupino, for example), Scott has begged to differ from the theory that insists on Bogart's scrupulous professionalism: 'He set the pace,' she recalled. 'He would arrive on the set totally unprepared at nine. He would then proceed to learn his lines before his Martini and lunch. Then he would work till five and leave, the scene completed or not. These were his rules and although I was equally the star of the picture, I abided by them, as did the crew, the director, the producer and the studio.' Altogether *Dead Reckoning* was an unhappy experience, and although Bogart could now enjoy being able to call the shots – a position he clearly took every advantage of – the film itself was a good deal worse than much of the factory product that he had badmouthed so noisily during his apprenticeship at Warners.

Cromwell directs the bar-room scene.

Columbia's Dead Reckoning *poster, here offering convincing proof of the power of advertising. Lizabeth Scott's billing boasts 'You can't push me around' – but that is exactly what Bogart did.*

All Bogart's co-stars were equal . . .

. . . but some were more equal than others.

The Two Mrs Carrolls: *the artist at work.*

A few months later came *The Two Mrs Carrolls*, a film he had made with Barbara Stanwyck back in 1945 but which Warners had kept on the shelf for two years – probably for accounting reasons, although perhaps also because they did not think too highly of it. Most people who have written about Bogart consider it a disaster, but it is one of my favourites among his films. Adapted from a play by Martin Vale which had been a big hit during the Broadway season of 1943, it concerns a temperamental English artist, Geoffrey Carroll (played by Bogart), who settles down with his second wife (Stanwyck) in the improbably idyllic village of Ashton, where it always seems to be tea-time and the cathedral bells are continually chiming in the background. Soon a rumour starts getting around that Carroll murdered his first wife, shortly after doing a portrait of her as 'the Angel of Death', and when his second wife discovers that he has a similar picture of her stashed up in the attic – to say nothing of the smouldering looks he has been exchanging with his neighbour (Alexis Smith) over the cucumber sandwiches – she begins to suspect that her days as Mrs Carroll mark 2 might be numbered.

Although the screenplay does find an excuse for Bogart to put on his trench-coat and slug somebody, the main pleasure of the film – the reason it seems so much fresher than many of his forties productions – lies in seeing him relocated not only to an unfamiliar setting,

but also to an unfamilar genre, for *The Two Mrs Carrolls* has elements of the full-blooded 'women's picture' in the Bette Davis/Joan Fontaine mould. Of course, Bogart never convinces us for a moment that he is a talented painter (he handles his brushes about as comfortably as Claude Monet would have handled a Colt .45), but the film does strive towards an appreciation of the way in which artists – not just painters – use the people closest to them as sources of inspiration and might therefore be inclined to consider them disposable. There is a certain piquancy, too, in Bogart's playing a man who is desperately plotting to get rid of one wife in order to marry another, because the film was made in the early summer of 1945, at the very time when he was divorcing Mayo Methot and marrying Lauren Bacall. No wonder he seems to understand what Geoffrey Carroll is going through. It is Barbara Stanwyck, if anybody, who comes out of the movie badly: shamefully it fails to find an adequate part for one of the few actresses who might have stood up to Bogart on equal terms.

He and Bacall now made another film together, a disappointing thriller called *Dark Passage* which had the advantage of good location shooting in San Francisco but was laboriously plotted, ending as it does with an explanation speech from Bogart that is so tedious and long-winded that you wonder how audiences at the time, without the benefit of pause controls or rewind buttons, could ever have made head or tail of it. He plays a prisoner in San Quentin who has been framed for murder but escapes in order to prove his innocence. The gimmick is that the audience does not see his face until sixty minutes into the film: the escape sequence is shot entirely from Bogart's subjective point of view, and then, having undergone plastic surgery to give himself a new appearance, he wanders around wrapped up in bandages for half an hour. Disbelief becomes hard to suspend at this point:

Checking out the book of the film.

Our first glimpse of Bogart's face in Dark Passage: *unbelievable, but good.*

why would any plastic surgeon worth his salt give his patient the features of Humphrey Bogart, complete with scarred mouth and heavy bags under the eyes? At least this gives Bacall the chance, when his work is revealed, to deliver the definitive verdict on the Bogart face: 'It's unbelievable – but it's good.' She also tells us in her autobiography that Bogart was particularly tense during the filming of *Dark Passage* because more and more of his hair was falling out (he had been wearing a toupee in

his films for some time). Vitamin deficiencies were diagnosed – the legacy of more than a decade of poor eating, bad sleeping and heavy drinking – and he began a course of injections and scalp treatments.

With this anxiety preying on their minds, in April 1947 the Bogarts flew out to Mexico to join the crew of *The Treasure of the Sierra Madre* at the village of San José Purua. Their flight was diverted to Veracruz because of fog and the plane landed only on the fourth

*Rehearsing a fight scene with Clifton
Young for* Dark Passage, *on location
in San Francisco. The cameraman is
Sid Hickox.*

Midway through a long day's shooting on Sierra Madre, *with John and Walter Huston.*

attempt, just before it ran out of fuel. It was an inauspicious start, and the shoot itself turned out to be testing for everyone.

Sierra Madre, based on a novel by B. Traven, was exactly the kind of project that appealed to John Huston, who had been wanting to make this film for six years: macho, hard-nosed, downbeat entertainment with a veneer of social comment, an exotic location (he was especially fond of Mexico) and vague leftist overtones. Traven himself was a reclusive figure. Even his agent had never met him, and although most people believed that the 'translator' who called himself Hal Croves and who acted as a technical adviser on the film, was in fact Traven all along, Huston was never convinced. Everything about the venture was risky, from Hollywood's point of view, and Jack Warner could hardly believe that he had allowed himself to be talked into putting up nearly three million dollars for a film to be made almost entirely on location outside the United States – especially when the daily rushes began to be shipped back and he saw that Huston was turning Bogart, who had finally emerged as the studio's top romantic lead, into a grizzled, unshaven slob driven by a mixture of paranoia and greed.

The film gave Huston plenty of scope to indulge his penchant for finding difficult locations, with a cavalier disregard for the comfort of his cast and crew. Bogart complained that 'John wanted everything perfect. I have to

admire him for that but it was plenty rough on our troupe. If we could get to a location site without fording a couple of streams and walking through rattlesnake-infested areas in the scorching sun, then it wasn't quite right.' To compound the problem, the location catering was a disaster and Bacall had to step in, ordering large quantities of canned soup, meat and beans and supervising the preparation of the food herself.

It was also on the set of *Sierra Madre* that Bogart and Huston had their first major quarrel. Earlier in the year Bogart had realized a

With Bacall on location for Dark Passage.

In Pasadena, California, four days after their wedding. On her wrist Bacall is wearing a present from Bogie – a memento of her famous challenge from To Have and Have Not: 'You know how to whistle, don't you, Steve? You just put your lips together and . . . blow.'

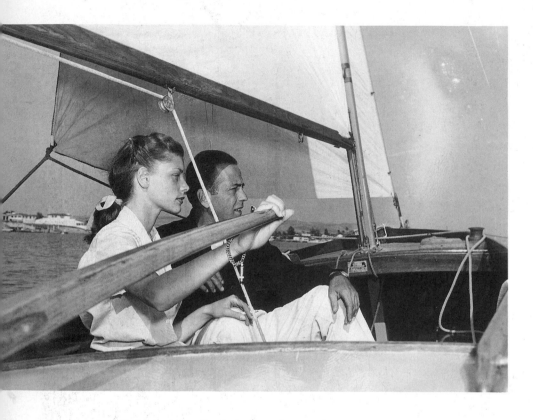

Sailing with Bacall, who looks nearly as enthusiastic about yachts as she did about chess.

Most of the advertising for Sierra Madre *tried to give the impression that it was an action picture.*

lifelong dream and bought himself a racing yacht, called the *Santana*. Bacall has said that 'when Bogie bought that boat he was enslaved – happily so – and truly had everything he'd ever dreamed of . . . If ever I had a woman to be jealous of, she was the *Santana*.' He was adamant that he was going to enter the boat in that year's Honolulu race, and Huston was equally adamant that he was going to stay in Mexico until shooting on the film was completed. Although most accounts of this argument treat it as having been rather comic, at root there was something deadly serious at stake for both men: Bogart's first love was always the sea, and Huston, for all his vagaries, was a dedicated film-maker determined to get the best out of his material. Relations deteriorated as the date of the race got nearer and nearer, and one night, unable to stand Bogart's nagging any longer – 'Out to make a fucking masterpiece, right, John?' – Huston grabbed him by the nose and twisted until tears came into his eyes. The entire table went silent; then Bacall said, 'John, you're hurting him.' 'Yes, I know. I mean to,' Huston answered. After that, shooting continued for as long as he wanted, including two extra weeks in Bakersfield, California.

Jack Warner's opinion of *Sierra Madre* went through a reversal when he saw the finished version. On 1 August 1947 he sent a wire to his general sales manager in New York:

DEAR BENNY: THIS IS THE FIRST TIME I HAVE EVER DONE THIS BUT LAST NIGHT I RAN, IN 12,500 FEET, THE TREASURE OF THE SIERRA MADRE. I WANT YOU AND THOSE ASSEMBLED TO KNOW THIS IS DEFINITELY THE GREATEST MOTION PICTURE WE HAVE EVER MADE . . . A FEW YEARS BACK THIS ONE PICTURE WOULD VIRTUALLY PUT OVER A WHOLE SEASON'S PRODUCT. THAT'S THE SIZE OF IT.

The film presented a problem, all the same, to Warners' advertising department, since it fitted into none of the existing genres. They ended up promoting it more or less as a Western, and Bogart, who was the only big star in the whole production, was roped into a campaign that had him endorsing a line of smart men's clothing, none of it remotely resembling the costumes he had worn as Fred C. Dobbs. It was to no avail, in any case, because the film still did badly at the box office.

For all its reputation, *The Treasure of the Sierra Madre* is a surprisingly tedious film to watch. This is partly to do with its monotonous visual texture – Huston was determined to glamorize neither the characters nor the locale – but it is also the fault of the film's rather simple-minded morality. After slightly more than two hours the audience comes away having learned (a) that man is inherently greedy and (b) that greed leads to dissatisfaction and unhappiness. Neither of these insights seems worthy of the portentousness and care with which the story has been put on screen. (I use the word 'man' advisedly, because woman barely rates a walk-on part in this movie.) As for Bogart, it is frustrating that the part of Dobbs didn't stretch him more; the star turn of the film is provided by Walter Huston as the senior prospector Howard, and Bogart's performance doesn't really hit full stride until the final scenes, when he starts breaking down and speaking to himself in cracked, fearful monologues:

> Curtin didn't cry when I shot him. Not a sound out of him. He just dropped like a tree falls . . . Funny the way his arms and legs were twisted around. I could have laughed right out. [*Chuckles.*] Just to think, one slug and finished. A whole life. [*Chuckles again.*] Tiger got him all right. Took him up in his jaws and carried him off. Must have been a big tiger – a royal tiger. They can jump over a fence with a cow in their mouths.

Dobbs is essentially an extension of the unsympathetic parts Bogart used to trot out for gangster movies, except that the script furnishes him with more in the way of motivation, by stressing the corrupting effects of poverty, and also adds an undertone of incipient paranoia. It is a measure of Bogart's growth as an actor that not only is he equal to this material, but also – however sophisticated it may seem when compared with some of his

As Dobbs in The Treasure of the Sierra Madre.

other parts – he is starting to look constrained by it.

Hollywood was now entering a phase during which films like *The Treasure of the Sierra Madre* would be even harder to make. No sooner was World War II over than America went through its notorious ideological shift, from jingoistic anti-fascism to mindless anti-communism, and strong pressures were brought into play to discourage people from making films that dealt with poverty, or with 'the common man', or that had the temerity to imply that life in the USA was anything less than hunky-dory. At the centre of this movement – the precursor of full-blown McCarthyism – was a congressman called J. Parnell Thomas. In May 1947, with the support of the right-wing Motion Picture Alliance for the Preservation of American Ideals, which drew up for his perusal a list of allegedly 'subversive' movies, Thomas moved his House Un-American Activities Committee (HUAC) into a hotel in Los Angeles to begin its investigation into communist infiltration of the film industry. In closed session, he heard the testimony of fourteen co-operative witnesses – including Gary Cooper, Robert Taylor and Jack Warner – and on the basis of their information he subpoena'd nineteen directors, actors, producers and writers to appear before a public committee in Washington in October. They included Lewis Milestone, Ring Lardner Jr, Bertolt Brecht, Howard Koch (co-writer of *Casablanca*), Robert Rossen (co-writer of *Marked Woman* and *The Roaring Twenties*) and Edward Dmytryk (who went on to direct Bogart in *The Caine Mutiny*).

Hollywood's liberals, outraged by this assault on their independence, mounted a counter-attack and set up a Committee for the First Amendment (CFA) under the leadership of John Huston, William Wyler and the screenwriter Philip Dunne. The idea was that when the nineteen witnesses were asked the key question – 'Are you now or have you ever been a member of the Communist party?' – they would refuse to answer, pleading freedom of belief under the First Amendment to the Constitution and pointing out that no committee of Congress had the right to inquire into a citizen's political affiliations. Shortly before the public hearings were due to begin, calls were made to the CFA by several of the 'Unfriendly Nineteen' and the lawyers representing them, suggesting that a party of sympathetic celebrities be assembled and sent up to Washington in order to give moral support and to attract publicity. Howard Hughes offered to provide them with a private plane, and among the stars who made the journey were Danny Kaye, Gene Kelly, Paul Henreid, Sterling Hayden and, of course, the Bogarts. Bogart himself released a statement in which he said that 'It's none of my business who's a communist and who isn't', but at the same time 'I am an outraged and angry citizen who

Bogart, Bacall and other liberal sympathizers (including Paul Henreid, Gene Kelly and Marsha Hunt) set off for Washington to register their disapproval of the HUAC investigations.

Bacall, Bogart and John Huston in serious frame of mind on the set of Key Largo.

feels that my civil liberties are being taken away from me'. Bacall wrote a longer and more fully argued front-page article for the *Washington Daily News*, warning readers, 'You have no idea of the fear that has overtaken Hollywood. A producer is afraid to produce, a director is afraid to direct, and a writer is afraid to write for fear anything he might say or do will be controversial to the point that he might be accused of the same thing that the witnesses who have been called here have been accused of. Which means in simple language that good adult entertainment flies out the window and shallow water flows in the door.'

It is well known that the HUAC hearings turned out to be a shambles. Huston had his own ideas about how the witnesses should conduct themselves before the committee, and suggested at a private meeting that they should respectfully decline to answer any questions about their membership of the Communist Party, but then offer to give a press conference at which they would answer any questions that reporters cared to put to them. In this way they would show that they had nothing to hide, but would have made the point that any official inquiry into their political beliefs was unconstitutional. Not only did the Nineteen choose not to adopt this strategy, but it wouldn't have done them any good anyway, since nobody had banked on J. Parnell Thomas's idiosyncratic methods of chairing a committee, which included never allowing anyone to answer in

more than one syllable, and constantly interrupting the witnesses by banging incessantly on his desk with a gavel. (Thomas was sent to jail for taking bribes and fiddling the payroll only two years later.) As successive witnesses took the stand and feebly attempted to turn their answers into direct attacks on the HUAC, the proceedings grew more and more heated and unproductive. The first ten were cited for contempt of court, the eleventh (Bertolt Brecht) denied membership – and left the country the next day – and the other hearings

were postponed. Nobody had emerged with any credit, and the press, which had earlier been generally supportive of the Nineteen, was now openly critical of the 'Unfriendly Ten' who had made it to the witness stand. Huston could see why: 'It was a sorry performance. You felt your skin crawl and your stomach turn. I disapproved of what was being done to the Ten, but I also disapproved of their response. They had lost a chance to defend a most important principle.'

Huston and the Bogarts returned from

Conferring with Evelyn Keyes and Danny Kaye in the Presidential Room of the National Airport after arriving in Washington.

Washington demoralized, but determined to continue working within the system without giving up their beliefs. Assigned by Warners to direct a screen adaptation of Maxwell Anderson's portentous blank-verse play, *Key Largo*, Huston decided to make it into both a starring vehicle for Bogart and an allegory of resurgent fascism. He turned the central character, Frank McCloud, into a World War II veteran returning to America only to find that the very evils against which he has been fighting – gangsterism, bullying, paranoia and illiberalism in general – are back in the ascendant. The personification of these qualities is one Johnny Rocco (played by Edward G. Robinson), a gangster on his way down to Cuba who takes over a small hotel in Key Largo and holds the family hostage. Prominent among his disagreeable attributes is a knee-jerk hatred of communism: 'After being in the United States for more than thirty years, they called me an undesirable alien. Me – Johnny Rocco! Like I was a dirty Red or something.' When the hotel owner (Lionel Barrymore) describes Rocco as 'filth', McCloud responds with sarcasm: 'Oh, Mr Temple, you're hopelessly old-fashioned. Your ideas date back years. You're still living in

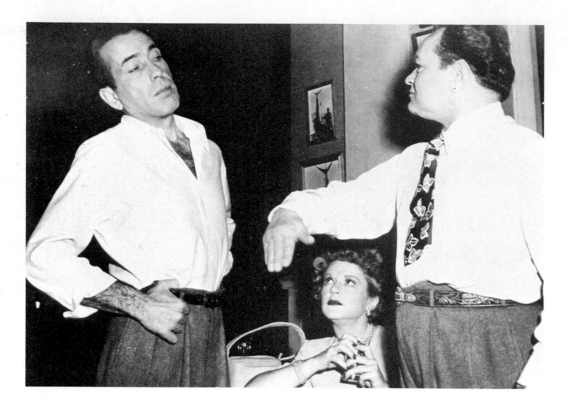

*Taking a punch from Edward G.
Robinson as Claire Trevor looks on.*

Key Largo: *their fourth and final
screen partnership.*

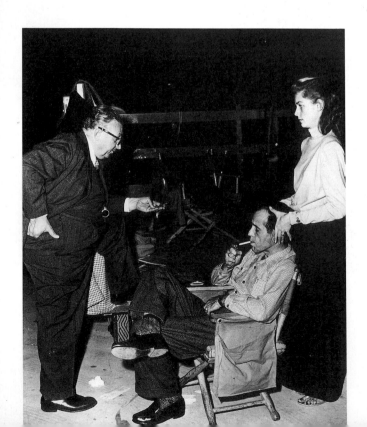

On the Key Largo *set with director of photography Karl Freund, veteran of many American and European films, including Fritz Lang's* Metropolis.

the time when America thought it could get along without the Johnny Roccos. Welcome back, Rocco, it was all a mistake. America's sorry for what it did to you.'

The leading part was so obviously tailored for Bogart that he doesn't have to put much effort into it. Like Rick, and like Harry Morgan, McCloud is at first neutral and self-interested, in the face of the threat posed by Rocco ('I fight nobody's battles but my own,' he says, in the umpteenth variation on this sentiment); but then, spurred on by adoring looks from Bacall, his finer feelings spring into action and he ends up giving the gangsters a lift on a local boat and bumping them off one by one. This climax, incidentally, is taken directly from the final chapters of Hemingway's *To Have and Have Not*, which were never used in Howard Hawks's film.

The fact that Huston allowed McCloud's boat to be called the *Santana* typifies the spirit of mutual admiration and camaraderie in which *Key Largo* was made. The cast and crew were largely made up of friends and be-leaguered liberal sympathizers: Bacall would serve tea in her dressing room while Lionel Barrymore and Edward G. Robinson entertained everyone with theatrical stories. These few months must have come as a relief to Robinson, who was by now almost unemployable thanks to the wild rumours that were flying around about his membership of the Communist Party and his possible secret life as a

Russian agent. Although they were never close friends, Bogart unfailingly deferred to the senior actor, calling him down to the set each morning with a gentle knock on his dressing-room door; and he was happy, too, to let Robinson get bigger billing in the credits and advertisements for the film.

Soon after shooting was completed, however, relations between the two actors soured slightly. With media attitudes and public opinion becoming rapidly less tolerant, any actors of known liberal tendencies – particularly those associated with the behaviour of the 'Unfriendly Ten' – stood in danger of losing popularity and jeopardizing their careers. The temptation for them to distance themselves from any taint of communism was strong, and while Robinson was to hold out for a few more years yet, Bogart was one of the first to crack, making self-justifying statements for *Newsweek* and *Photoplay*. 'I detest communism just as any decent American does,' he said. 'That the trip [to Washington] was ill-advised, even foolish, I am ready to admit. I am an American and very likely, like a good many of the rest of you, sometimes a foolish and impetuous American.'

This recantation seems graceless and unnecessary, coming as it did at a time when the right to freedom of belief had never stood in need of stouter defence. It raises the question of whether Bogart's political convictions, which were partly a product of the liberalism

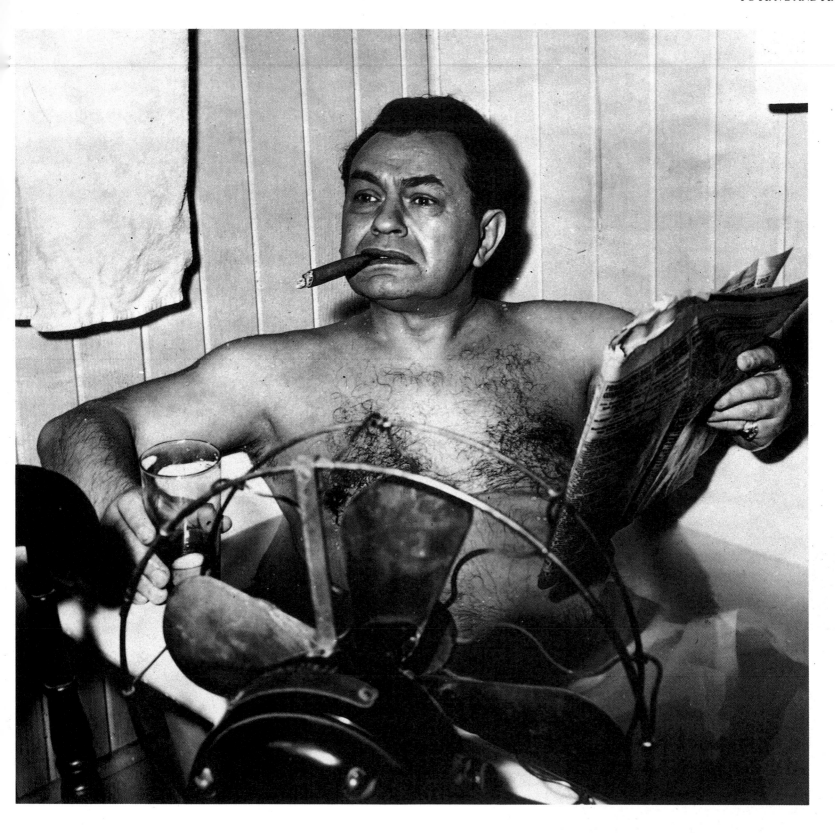

Robinson makes a memorable first appearance in Key Largo.

Bacall, Bogart, Skitch Henderson and Bill Stern open the 1952 Eisenhower election campaign at Madison Square Garden. Soon after this Bacall switched her allegiance to Adlai Stevenson, the Democratic candidate, and persuaded Bogart to follow her.

he had absorbed during the theatrical thirties (when it was at its most fashionable), were really strong enough to stand up under pressure. It is true that he has been described as an 'ardent Democrat', and that he made a campaign broadcast for Roosevelt in 1944, subsequently defending his action (actors were supposed to keep out of politics) in an article for the *Saturday Evening Post* headlined 'I stuck my neck out'. And Hoagy Carmichael has related how a drunken Bogart once abused him loudly at a party for his Republican sympathies, in an argument that was about to degenerate into a fist fight until Carmichael's wife intervened. ('Humphrey Bogart was a bit confused politically' was his regretful conclusion.) On the other hand, British readers need to remember that the two American political parties are scarcely polarized. In an old *Beyond*

the Fringe sketch about America, it was observed that 'they've inherited our two-party system. They have the Republican Party – which is the equivalent of our Conservative Party – and they have the Democratic Party – which is the equivalent of our Conservative Party.' Indeed, in the 1952 election campaign Bogart was all set to vote for Eisenhower, and this without any noticeable shift in his political position; it was only the insistent persuasion of Bacall that brought him back to Adlai Stevenson and the Democrat cause. In fact during the last years of his life it may have been Bacall, whose beliefs were a product of her considerably less privileged background, who helped to keep his leftism alive.

This is confirmed by a revealing story told by David McLure, who for a long time was the assistant, or 'legman', to the influential and

maniacally right-wing gossip columnist Hedda Hopper. (She was prone to refer to MGM, for instance, as 'Metro-Goldwyn-Moscow'.) Hopper looked on Bogart's politics with horror, and once named him as one of 'the four most dangerous men in America' – prompting Bacall to remark laconically, 'I think it's time for Hedda to shut up.' Hopper felt so pleased and vindicated when Bogart distanced himself from the 'Unfriendly Ten' that she made a point of mentioning it on her radio show, but McLure, recalling the incident, believed that 'So much of it was surface. Take Bogart. There was the political thing, but Bogie wasn't really political. Bogie without Bacall was a pretty goddamn good Joe. Bogie was a drunk who was liable to take offence and say any goddamn thing. On her radio program, Hopper had a feature, "My Hat's Off", and for some goddamn reason it was off to Bogie. They'd had these political differences. Bogie was drunk and called up and said, "I don't want her taking her hat off to me." I told Hopper, and the next day she called him. I was listening on the other phone, and . . . he was very contrite about it. He was a belligerent drunk, but he couldn't retain anger very long. You see you're dealing in a world of shallow emotions. There are fireworks. And by the time you or I get interested in the whole damn thing it's over. So unless you catch this feature, you can't explain these people. Because they're not normal people at all.'

Attending the Key Largo *première.*

5

THE ENFORCER

independence, 1948-53

Towards the end of the 1940s Bogart made two different ventures into production. The first was the setting up of his independent film company, the Santana Pictures Corporation; the second was the fathering of his son, Stephen Humphrey Bogart, who was born on 6 January 1949.

Santana – named after Bogart's beloved yacht – was formed on 7 April 1948. Bogart had gone into business with Mark Hellinger, with whom he hoped to make the one independent movie a year to which he was entitled under his Warner Brothers contract. He already owned forty-five per cent of the Hellinger Corporation, and when Hellinger died in 1947 (at the age of only forty-four), Bogart bought up the rest of the stock and became sole owner. He appointed Robert Lord producer and negotiated a deal with Columbia that gave him complete control over production, while the studio would help with the financing and distribution of the films.

It was an opportunity he had been hungering after for years. After all the frustrations of working on Warners' production line, the seemingly endless succession of undemanding or unsuitable parts, this was a chance to call the shots, to choose scripts that reflected his own values and could be carefully tailored to fit his developing but in many ways circumscribed resources as an actor. He could choose his own directors and his own co-stars: he would no longer have to 'take it and like it'. The lame-ness of three out of the first four Santana films therefore says a good deal about the limited extent to which Bogart ever understood the nature of his particular strengths and weaknesses.

The first fruit of this new enterprise, *Knock on Any Door*, had a certain potential. Based on a novel by Willard Motley, it offers itself as a sympathetic study of juvenile delinquency, with Bogart starring as a big-time lawyer, Andrew Morton, who takes on the defence of a teenage offender from the slums, played by John Derek (the same John Derek who went on to marry Bo and direct her in such soft-porn milestones as *Tarzan the Ape Man* and *Bolero*). It was directed by Nicholas Ray, whose career

With John Derek in Knock on Any Door.

had got off to a good start with two well-received features for RKO. Bogart at this time was still regarded in some corners of Holly-wood as a drunk and a troublemaker, and Ray once recalled getting a phone call from a well-wishing friend who asked him, 'Hey, Nick, what the hell are you doing? You've got a good start on your career and now you're making a film with one of the biggest lushes in town.' He replied carelessly, 'I guess that's my problem, isn't it?' and afterwards found little to complain of in Bogart's professional standards. 'Bogart did have a problem,' he conceded, 'and could only work through six takes, the same scene six times, before he'd dry up.' The real difficulty with *Knock on Any Door*, though, lies not in the performances but in the script: the young delinquent, Nick Romano, is clearly the most interesting character – as well as being exactly the kind of mixed-up, antisocial outsider whom Ray would usually make the focus of his films – but the conception of the movie as a starring vehicle for Bogart forces a disproportionate amount of attention on to the character of Morton, and this is the cue for some big courtroom speeches that drag things down into preachiness. The film is fondly remembered, all the same, for one line which has become a classic: 'Live fast, die young and leave a good-looking corpse.'

To the second and fourth Santana films, *Tokyo Joe* (1949) and *Sirocco* (1951), silence is the only charitable response. Both were wretchedly ill-considered attempts to re-create the success of *Casablanca*, with Bogart doing his disillusioned anti-hero number first as a night-club proprietor in Tokyo and then as a gun-runner in Damascus. Both suffer from implausible plots, thin characterizations and incredibly murky lighting, and are paced so slowly that audiences might well find themselves wondering whether the projector is running at the right speed.

To see these films is to realize that the typical Bogart persona, which made him the cult hero of American campuses and the existential darling of French film criticism, was not entirely of his own making but depended to a very large extent on the input of a series of talented writers and directors: one might point to John Huston, Mark Hellinger, Casey Robinson, Howard Hawks, Jules Furthman, William Faulkner, Leigh Brackett, W.R. Burnett and Raoul Walsh as having been instrumental in this respect. Bogart's assumption that he could go it alone, sustaining the appeal himself with only a minimum of back-up from a team of carelessly chosen and undistinguished collaborators, seems naïve. The winter of 1950/51 found him falling back once again on his Rick/Harry Morgan impersonation. This time the medium was radio.

Like most Hollywood stars, Bogart had been featured on radio throughout the forties in adaptations of his most popular movies, among them *Bullets or Ballots, High Sierra,*

Bogart has his first taste of parenthood: baby Steve is about four months old, his father getting on for fifty.

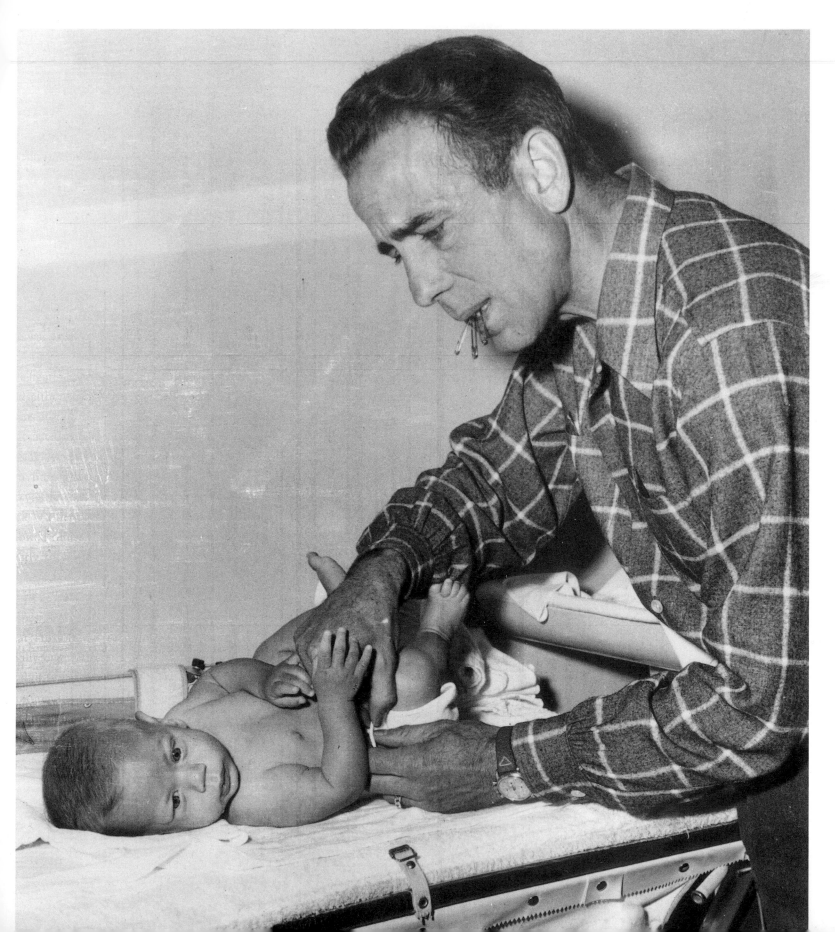

Making a radio broadcast with Bacall.

Casablanca and *The Maltese Falcon* (in which Bacall took the part of Brigid O'Shaughnessy). He had also done some original work, such as a 1945 play, *Love's Lovely Counterfeit* by James M. (*Double Indemnity*) Cain, and a sixty-minute version of Hemingway's *A Farewell to Arms*, playing opposite Joan Fontaine. Now he took the initiative and starred with Bacall in a series called *Bold Venture*, set in a seedy hotel in Havana. He was Slate Shannon, the hotel's proprietor; she was Sailor Duvall, a young woman placed by her dying father under Shannon's protection. The plots frequently centred around his boat, the *Bold Venture* of the title, often necessitating sound effects of lapping waves and outboard motors chugging into action. The series brought them a fair amount of money – some $4,000 a week – but was not otherwise successful, since the scripts, by Morton Fine and David Friedkin, never took fire; but nostalgia for Bogart was strong enough after his death for a TV adaptation to be mounted, and this was a modest hit in the late fifties.

Meanwhile, August 1950 brought the release of the third Santana film, *In a Lonely Place*, which ranks as one of Bogart's masterpieces. It was again directed by Nicholas Ray, but this time with a level of feeling and commitment that consistently illuminates its investigation of the psychology of violence. In fact this is the only one of Bogart's films that gets anywhere near the heart of this subject, because the issue here is not clouded over by the qualifying conventions of the gangster movie. He plays Dixon Steele, a Hollywood screenwriter who has been highly regarded in the past but now finds himself out of work, scuppered both by his contempt for the industry's values and by his reputation for sudden, volatile flashes of temper. As the film opens, his agent tracks him down to a bar and hands him a trashy bestselling novel, saying that he can have the job of adapting it if he can read it tonight and present his ideas by tomorrow morning. By good luck, the hat-check girl at the bar has read the book and offers to come back to his apartment and tell him the story. She leaves the apartment in the early hours of the morning, and the next day is found murdered. Suspicion falls on Steele, although he is provided with something approaching an alibi by his neighbour, Laurel Gray (played by Gloria Grahame), with whom he goes on to have an affair which at last untaps his creative abilities. But the doubt still lingers in her mind – whenever she sees how unpredictable and

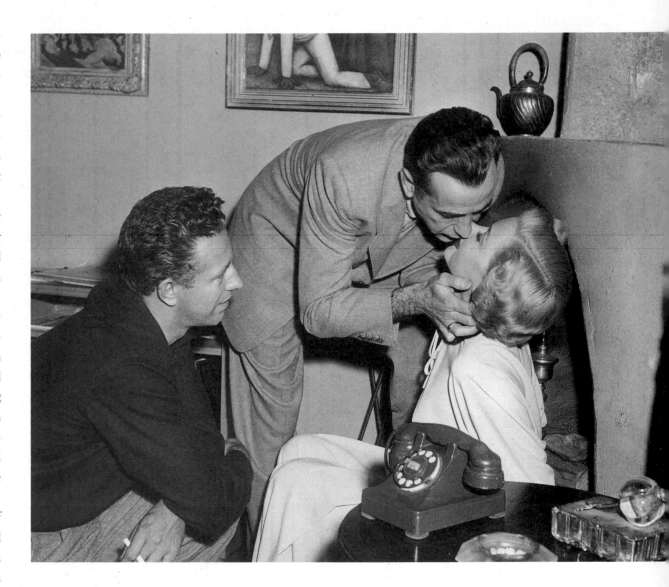

Getting detailed instructions on how to kiss Gloria Grahame from her husband, director Nicholas Ray.

141

Looking more than usually wasted in
In a Lonely Place, *the film that*
touches parts the other Bogart films
were afraid to reach.

irascible he can be – that he might have committed the murder.

The disclosing of Steele's malevolence is superbly orchestrated: Ray teases it out, piece by piece. At first it is just the way Bogart throws his shoes off at night, making the hat-check girl start involuntarily; later, his abrupt stubbing-out of a cigarette on the lid of a piano causes a bar-room chanteuse to miss her stroke. Then there is the relish in his voice as he describes what it must feel like to strangle someone: '. . . bulging eyes and protruding tongue . . . Squeeze harder. It's wonderful to feel her throat crush under your arm.' Finally he explodes when he has a run-in with a young driver, his anger already at a pitch following a disastrous beach party; the beating that he metes out, and the crazed, almost ecstatic light in his eyes, are more shocking and unexpected than anything else in Bogart's work. The lonely place at which he has arrived, by this stage, is not the deserted roadside where the murder was carried out but a bleak, wounded isolationism which leads to his separation from Grahame and finally lends, against all odds, a genuine grandeur to the film's melancholy refrain: 'I was born when she kissed me. I died when she left me. I lived a few weeks while she loved me.'

'It's hard to tell what Dix Steele feels about anything,' says an old army colleague. 'None of us could ever figure him out.' This is the sinister flipside of Sam Spade's emotional

reticence and of Rick's dogged neutrality: suppose these qualities concealed, not the heroism that is always waiting to be drawn out by a good woman or a tight corner, but a real viciousness, a real violence? The question has to be asked about Bogart himself, because he is very, very good as Dixon Steele and, as Raymond Chandler once remarked, 'Bogart is always good at playing Bogart.' In fact the film goes out of its way to tighten the analogies between Bogart and Steele, from having Steele

dine out on ham and eggs (Bogart's own regular order at Romanoff's), to providing him with a drunken pal – a bit like the Walter Brennan character in *To Have and Have Not* – who not only is the sort of eccentric companion Bogart liked to have around in real life, but is actually played by Robert Warwick, an old friend from the Playhouse Theatre days who was in the cast of Bogart's very first play, *Drifting*.

How much of Dixon Steele, then, was

In a Lonely Place. *Dixon Steele's temper gets the better of him again.*

MAGISTRATES COURT
SUMMONS PART

Bogart leaves a central Manhattan court in September 1949, following the dismissal of a third-degree assault charge.

there in Bogart? A story told by Lauren Bacall sounds as though it could be about either character. She recalls an evening shortly before their marriage when they were together on his boat: 'I don't know what happened this time – when or how the click in his brain took place – but suddenly he was fighting with me. I got more and more frightened. He started slamming his fists on the table, crying, "You goddamn actresses are all alike." The more I tried to cajole and pacify him, the worse he got . . . I'd never seen fury like his – unreasonable, lashing out. I hated it.'

There is no doubt that Bogart's aggression was alcohol-related. Medical practitioners like to distinguish between alcoholism – where the body exhibits a genuine chemical dependency – and 'problem drinking', which is probably what he suffered from. Outbreaks of savagery like this were relatively rare, and they tailed off as his marriage to Bacall sorted itself out and he found himself needing the drink less badly (although he never came anywhere close to giving it up). He continued, though, to leave behind him a trail of stories about beating up cab drivers and picking fights at parties and

being thrown out of night-clubs. In its milder manifestation, this pugilism took the form of his legendary 'needling', an issue on which the entire Hollywood community seems to have been divided: some saw it as a praiseworthy exercise in deflating pomposity, others found it boorish and insulting. He has been praised for his 'brinkmanship' (the art of bringing an argument to the point of physical violence and then backing down), and it's true that there are no stories – none at all – of his ever having *won* a fight with anybody. Conflicting theories have been put forward to account for his obsession with this form of conversation, but it seems likely (as one might expect with someone who had struggled so unsuccessfully with his career during the lean years of the twenties and thirties) that there was a large element of the persecution complex in Bogart's character. On screen he was often wooden and unconvincing as a tough guy, after all, but he never once gave a bad performance as a paranoiac.

'I took the gun out of Bogie's hands,' said Nick Ray of *In a Lonely Place*, joining the swelling ranks of writers and directors who claim to have revolutionized his career. Perhaps it is true that he alone took the gun out of Bogart's hands *and* made a good film out of it. In any case, Warner Brothers lost no time in putting the gun back into his hands by casting him as *The Enforcer*, District Attorney Martin Ferguson, who has the tricky job of breaking up a powerful murder-for-profit organization after all the key witnesses have been eliminated. This is a taut and suspenseful movie, fairly horrific in its implied violence (especially the scene where one victim gets his throat cut in a barber's shop), and tapping in to some of the malevolence that Bogart had recently revealed in his portrayal of Dixon Steele: Ferguson's methods of interrogation, for instance, include cynically victimizing his suspect's wife and child. The density of the plot, which is based on a true story, does not allow his performance much room to breathe, and this is one of the few Bogart films where it is possible to believe – as you couldn't with *High Sierra*, say, or *The Big Sleep* – that it might have been just as good with a different star in the central role. The final ten minutes generate the sort of tension that we associate with Hitchcock rather than Bogart, so praise for the movie's success should go to the director: not Bretaigne Windust, the man credited in the titles, but Raoul Walsh, who apparently did most of the work.

The reputation of a particular film – the extent to which it gets written about and discussed – depends more often than not on external factors such as the circumstances that attached to its production. In this way, modest, efficient films like *The Enforcer* tend to get overlooked – a fact that rarely befalls the work of John Huston, whose approach to directing seems to have been purposely developed to provide an inexhaustible fund of

Gun back in hand as District Attorney Martin Ferguson in The Enforcer.

Bogart and Bacall in Venice on the Italian leg of their European trip, prior to filming The African Queen.

anecdotes for biographers and historians.

The stories surrounding the making of *The African Queen* are now almost as well known as the film itself. Huston and Lauren Bacall have both written accounts of the experience; Katharine Hepburn devoted a whole book to it; and there can be few people, in the wake of Clint Eastwood's film *White Hunter, Black Heart*, who are unaware of the tensions provoked during shooting by Huston's unpredictable behaviour – and by his tendency to regard the whole film as an excuse to go to Africa and live out his Hemingway-style fantasies of becoming a big-game hunter.

It was not an easy project to set up from the very beginning. The rights to C.S. Forester's novel were owned by Warner Brothers, who had once toyed with the idea of building it into a vehicle for Bette Davis; they had bought it from Columbia, who had been planning to cast Elsa Lanchester and Charles Laughton in the Hepburn and Bogart roles. Huston and producer Sam Spiegel now bought the rights for $50,000, and struck up a deal with a British company, Romulus films, who were to provide the sterling necessary to finance the location work in Africa (although eventually it was shot in the Belgian Congo, which meant that most of the money had to be changed into Belgian francs). Bogart agreed to do it because he wanted to work with Hepburn; Hepburn, because she wanted to work with Bogart. Both stars agreed to take deferred salaries (as did

Huston) in order to get the film made.

Bogart and Bacall left their two-year-old son in the care of a nanny and embarked upon what was to turn into a four-and-a-half-month trip. Their first stops were in Paris, London and Rome, and for Bogart – at the age of fifty-one – it was his first experience of these cities. He was followed everywhere not only by fans but by the press – even, much to his surprise, when they made the first leg of their African

Looking on sceptically as Hepburn, a near-teetotaller, tries to convince him of the virtues of milk.

journey and arrived at Léopoldville. By this stage they had met up with Katharine Hepburn, who was travelling on her own and seemed understandably nervous about the whole enterprise. On her brief meetings with Huston she had found him wayward and exasperating, and she was worried that he and Bogart, in combination, would be too much to handle. While she took an immediate liking to the Bogarts, she was conscious that even after

the crew. Hepburn observed admiringly that he never seemed to sweat, and towards the end of the filming, when people were going down with dysentery and every other sort of stomach problem, he remained in good health – probably because he kept well clear of the local water, even to the extent of brushing his teeth in whiskey. (What this must have done to his teeth is another matter.) He was, however, deeply ill at ease in Africa, and he both envied and resented Hepburn's perpetual cheerfulness and resilience. 'At the end of the day he was tired,' she recalled. 'So until he'd had a drink or two he was grumpy. He'd come to the table and sort of begin to needle me. I was adorable and malleable and well-trained to handle the male grumps. I just agreed with everything he said. Then he'd smooth out. He was an extraordinarily decent fellow. Fair – forthright – uncomplicated.'

As shooting progressed, Bogart became progressively more anxious to return to civilization. Matters were not improved when a letter arrived from Lauren Bacall's mother, enclosing a newspaper clipping announcing that Mayo Methot had finally died, alone in a motel, following a long illness brought on by alcoholism. His only comment was 'Too bad. Such a waste' – referring, apparently, to her career, for he remained convinced of her gifts as an actress. Filming, which had begun on the Ruiki river, moving to Butiaba for the village scenes, finally took the cast to the Murchison

six years of marriage they radiated an intense privacy: 'She and Bogie seemed to have the most enormous opinion of each other's charms, and when they fought it was with the utter confidence of two cats locked deliciously in the same cage.'

This uneasy threesome now made their way to Stanleyville, where they were supposed to rendezvous with Huston – only to find that he had left for Bionda, where shooting was to begin, just an hour before they arrived. Hep-

burn was beside herself with fury at what she saw as the director's insensitivity. Bogart was resigned and unsurprised. He took the opportunity to warn Bacall not to be seduced by Huston's adventurism: in her own words, 'Bogie made it clear that I was going on no shoot with John, who, he maintained, could not hit his hat. Bogie disliked the idea of killing animals anyway.'

Physically, Bogart coped with the rigours of Africa better than just about anyone else on

In British Uganda, proudly displaying an eighty-pound perch. Bacall's more modest smile hides the fact that it was she who caught it.

*Survivors. Bacall, Bogie and
Hepburn arrive back in London in
July 1951.*

Reunited with Steve.

Relations among the African Queen company shifted as the filming progressed: Hepburn and Huston in particular developed an unexpected rapport.

Falls, where relations with Huston degenerated still further: Bogart was furious to be asked to put in an extra day's work when Steve had already been booked on a flight to London, where he was to be reunited with his parents.

Interestingly, by this time a shift seems to have taken place in the power relations among the *African Queen* company. At first Bogart and Huston considered Hepburn (who was a near-teetotaller) to be impossibly prim, and went out of the way to confirm her apprehensions about themselves. 'Both Bogie and I teased Katie unmercifully at the beginning,' Huston recalled. 'She thought we were rascals, scamps, rogues. We did everything we could to support this belief. We pretended to get roaring drunk. We even wrote dirty words in soap on her mirror.' It is hardly surprising, then, that Hepburn's first impression was of 'two over-male men'. But as she came to realize his strengths as a director, and after accompanying him on one of his hunting trips, she began to form a bond with Huston which left Bogart feeling isolated. In particular she shared his love of Africa and his manic commitment to the business of making the film as near perfect as possible, regardless of the physical hardships. It got to the point where Bogart believed she was 'aiding and abetting' Huston in his eccentricities.

By the time shooting finished, after eight weeks in Africa, the cast and crew of *The*

One of Hollywood's most memorable and unlikely screen romances.

Back in England, Bogart and Hepburn resumed work on The African Queen at Worton Hall Studios. It took another six weeks to finish making the film here.

African Queen had endured more than the pressures of constant ill-health: their camp had been invaded by ants; deadly black mamba snakes had been found in the toilet; torrential rain had delayed the filming; and the *African Queen* itself had sunk and been resurrected again. Early on, when they were still in Stanleyville, Hepburn and the Bogarts had been about to step into a fishing boat when it exploded and burst into flames; when the fire extinguisher failed to have any effect Hepburn was amazed to see that 'Bogie, completely courageous and cool, finally put it out by smothering it with the sand and a blanket. Right down in the fire he was, as far as I could see.' On the other hand – and despite the claims he made to the press at the time – Bogart's bravery did not extend to having his body covered in real leeches during the famous scene towards the end of the film. The scene was shot in a tank about four foot deep at Worton Hall Studios near London: his love of the ocean notwithstanding, Bogart hated swimming, and he nearly froze to death during the filming. Sadistic as ever, Huston let him believe that real leeches would have to be used – until the last minute, when he settled for a close-up of one leech on the chest of the breeder who had brought them into the studio. The rest of the day was spent trying to find some kind of rubber substitute that would look vaguely convincing and still cling to Bogart's wiry body. All day he had to sit there, naked from the waist up, while people planted various prototypes against his skin and assessed them for adhesiveness and authenticity.

Bogart's performance in this film grew in confidence as he overcame his distaste for Africa and his initial lack of rapport with Hepburn. John Huston has said that 'Bogie didn't particularly care for the Charlie Allnutt role when he started, but I slowly got him into it,

In the tank at Worton Hall. Before each scene, Hepburn recalled, it had to be cleared of buns which had been thrown in during the tea break.

A night out with two of the world's most beautiful women. Bogart doesn't seem to know which way to turn.

157

showing him by expression and gesture what I thought Allnutt should be like. He first imitated me, then all at once he got under the skin of that wretched, sleazy, absurd, brave little man. He realized he was on to something new and good. He said to me, "John, don't let me lose it. Watch me. Don't let me lose it."' It is arguable that in fact the affection in which this film is held by audiences has nothing to do with the credibility of the characters, but derives from a more knowing kind of enjoyment: the satisfaction of seeing Hollywood's most popular male and female stars – each of them evoking a whole range of rich and pleasurable associations – bringing great professionalism to bear on a charming, uncomplicated love story. There are few films where the question of credibility is less relevant. It is impossible to forget even for a moment that we are watching Hepburn and Bogart rather than a prissy English spinster and a Canadian low-life, and the Academy Award that Bogart won for the film seems to have been given less for this specific portrayal than as a cumulative tribute, an acknowledgement of his enduring presence and influence.

Once again, it seemed, John Huston had put him through hell and rewarded him with one of his more memorable movies, but for their final collaboration this arrangement was to be reversed: the filming of *Beat the Devil* in Italy was by all accounts sunny and harmonious, while the end result was, for Bogart at least, difficult to justify – especially as he had paid for it out of his own pocket.

Huston had lent him a copy of Claud Cockburn's novel (written under the pseudonym James Helvick) while they were filming *The African Queen*, and they both thought that they might be able to make another *Maltese Falcon*-style thriller out of it. Bogart bought the rights himself when he got back to America, and then busied himself with two more films for the major studios: *Deadline USA* and *Battle Circus*, both triumphantly mediocre movies which set the standard for the subsequent directing career of Richard Brooks. After these, Bogart decided to revive his Santana production company, engaged Huston as director for $175,000, and in February 1953 flew to London to check out the script that Peter Viertel and Tony Veiller had written for *Beat the Devil*.

Unhappy with their screenplay but financially committed to the picture, he moved on to Ravello, where the cast was beginning to assemble: it was a strong one, including Jennifer Jones, Gina Lollobrigida, Robert Morley and Peter Lorre. On the way, he and Huston were involved in a car crash when their chauffeur drove straight into a stone wall somewhere outside Rome: Bogart was thrown against the front seat and bit clean through his tongue, which he then had to have stitched up – without anaesthetic. (He seems, in general, to have had a high resistance to pain, as Hal Wal-

lis has testified in this gruesome anecdote: 'Although people have written that off screen Bogart was a soft and gentle man, I never found him so . . . He always wanted to seem as tough as possible. One night he met a man at a party who chewed glass in a circus, and Bogie smashed glasses and began to chew the pieces. His mouth was full of blood before he gave up.' Altogether this story says more for Bogie's courage than it does for his sense.)

Yet again, he found himself in a position where shooting on a film was to begin in a matter of days, without any sign of a usable script. At the suggestion of David O. Selznick they engaged the services of Truman Capote, who happened to be in Rome, to see what he could do with it. From then on Capote worked on his version of the script only a day or two ahead of shooting, while Huston was reduced to devising absurdly elaborate camera set-ups in order to kill time until the new pages arrived.

Legend has it that Capote completely rewrote *Beat the Devil*, and it has even been suggested that everyone was so unimpressed by the Viertel/Veiller script that a party was held three days before the picture began for the purpose of tearing it up. A comparison between their version and the completed film, however, shows that many of their ideas were retained. In particular, Capote followed their structure and arrangement of scenes almost exactly, his main contribution being to add more jokes and to rewrite the dialogue so that

Truman Capote, attending the première of another Gina Lollobrigida picture, Bread, Love and Dreams, *in New York.*

With Gina Lollobrigida *in* Beat the
Devil. *The stunning Italian locations
didn't quite compensate for the
inconsequentialities of plot.*

A donkey ride with Lollobrigida and Peter Lorre in Ravello helps to pass the time, while Capote is presumably in his hotel room writing the next scene.

the tone becomes vaguely camp and absurd, instead of sticking to the sort of macho wise-cracking with which Bogart might have felt more at ease. 'If you must know, I'm a typical rare spirit,' is not the kind of line that falls easily from his lips, although there are one or two more characteristic moments. 'The only thing standing between you and a watery grave is your wits,' he says to one adversary. 'It's not my idea of adequate protection.'

Strangely enough, he and Capote seem to have got on extremely well. Bogart and Huston did not normally feel comfortable with homosexuals – in fact throughout the shoot he kept up a nervous running joke that Capote and the director were having an affair – but he seems to have been captivated by this tough, charming, dapper little man, with his ankle-length overcoat and lavender scarf. In a letter to Bacall, he wrote, 'At first you can't believe him, he's so odd, and then you want to carry him around with you always.' Their friendship was cemented in an archetypal display of male bonding: an arm-wrestling match (which Capote won, twice), followed by a bear hug in which Capote tripped Bogart up so that he fell and fractured his elbow. 'I think that that in-cident, more than anything else, is what made us very good friends,' said the writer. 'After that he knew better than to fool around with me. I really liked Bogie. He was one of my all-time favourite people.' He also paid tribute to his working methods: 'He was really an artist

and a very selective one. All the gestures and expressions were pared down and pared down.'

However much Bogart may have liked him personally, he didn't approve of what Capote had done to the film, which subsequently did very badly in America and lost him a great deal of money. It baffled audiences who thought they knew what to expect from Bogart and Huston, and in this respect Jack Warner's

With Lollobrigida in Beat the Devil, *struggling to get to grips with the film's vein of camp comedy.*

Bogart and Robert Morley in Beat the Devil, *their second film together.*

response was fairly typical: 'There have been some Huston pictures you couldn't see with toothpicks propping your eyes open. One I particularly remember was *Beat the Devil*, filmed in Italy with Humphrey Bogart and Jennifer Jones. I think they shot it through beer-bottle glass instead of lenses.' For more open-minded viewers it is an unintentionally fascinating film, closer to the avant-garde than the mainstream in its wilful lack of interest in narrative, and curiously diffuse and static in its dependence on ensemble playing rather than a single star presence. Bogart was clearly the focal point around which the film was meant to be organized, but he seems to have been so confused by the whole rigmarole that he gives a totally blank performance, leaving a gaping hole at the centre of things which the livelier playing of Jones, Morley and Lorre serves to embellish rather than disguise. His inability to connect with the spirit of the film is confirmed by Robert Morley's recollection that while the rest of the cast would improvise ideas on the spot, Bogart's suggestions were rarely taken up with much enthusiasm. 'A nice man,' Morley concluded, 'but not very bright.'

Bogart seemed much happier with the middlebrow dramatics of *The Caine Mutiny*, in which he went on to star under the direction of Edward Dmytryk – one of the original 'Unfriendly Ten', who had recently served out his one-year prison sentence for contempt. Based on an inexplicably successful novel and

With his close friend and frequent co-star Peter Lorre, arriving in London in April 1953 after finishing work on Beat the Devil.

*As Captain Queeg on board the
USN* Caine.

*Bacall and Steve accompanied Bogart
to Honolulu for three weeks' location
work on* The Caine Mutiny.

Broadway play by Herman (*The Winds of War*) Wouk, it offered a juicy part for any actor in the shape of Captain Queeg, the hardline disciplinarian who takes charge of the dishevelled USN mine-sweeper *Caine* and shortly begins to display the symptoms of a dangerous paranoia, leaving Lieutenant Steve Meryk (Van Johnson) with no option but to relieve him of his command. Just about any actor in Hollywood would have been pleased to get this role: Dmytryk believes that 'casting tough-guy Humphrey Bogart as the psychotic and vulnerable Captain Queeg . . . was a stroke of near-genius, for which the producer, Stanley Kramer, deserves full credit', but the idea can hardly have been to cast completely against type, because Bogart was pretty much an old hand at playing this sort of unstable character, after *The Treasure of the Sierra Madre* and *In a Lonely Place*. In any case he was relieved, after his erratic experience of independent film-making, to be working with a big producer like Kramer, and with material that was more on his own wavelength.

Unfortunatley Dmytryk, however brave his politics, was an uninspired director and *The Caine Mutiny* suffers from garish colour, overbearing music and slack editing – not to mention Bogart's own observation that 'it was crapped up with an unnecessary love story'. 'It's a disappointment in my career, to tell the truth,' Dmytryk has said. 'I insist it could have been a classic.' This sounds fair enough, until

you hear what he actually means: 'The film should have been much longer. Stanley Roberts's original script was about 190 pages, even without the romantic subplot involving the ensign and the night-club singer. It should have remained that – a three-and-a-half- or four-hour picture.' Perish the thought. One of the main problems with the film was that in order to secure the use of aircraft carriers, destroyers and combat boats, the script had to be approved by the US Navy, who were outraged by the very suggestion that a mutiny might take place on one of their ships. At first they tried to get the title changed to *The Caine Incident*, then they insisted on an opening disclaimer saying that the events portrayed in the film could never happen in real life, and finally they asked for the character of Queeg to be toned down. In the final version it is implied that his paranoia is the result of battle fatigue, so paradoxically he emerges as the biggest hero of all. *The Caine Mutiny*, in this respect, was made just a little before its time: a few years later *Catch-22* and *Dr Strangelove* would start familiarizing everybody with the idea that paranoid psychosis is a perfectly normal state of mind for a commander in the American armed forces.

Bogart, at any rate, gave a magnificent performance, despite these restrictions – or perhaps even because of them, since the Navy's objections possibly forced him to find even subtler ways of hiding Queeg's neurosis beneath a veneer of buttoned-up efficiency. Fifteen years earlier at Warner Brothers, an unworthy vehicle such as this might have defeated him, but by now he was able to rise above it, transforming a simple-minded and manipulative potboiler into something moving and believable. Two sequences from the film are justly famous. One is the scene where Queeg is convinced that a member of his staff has pilfered some strawberries: to prove his point, he gets an officer to measure out, in sand, the exact amount of strawberries that everybody has had for dessert. The look of simultaneous watchfulness and quiet self-approval on Bogart's face, his gaze never leaving the measuring spoon for a second, shows beyond any doubt that he fully understood the art of acting with his eyes.

And then there is the courtroom scene, where Queeg's initial breezy assurance crumbles in the face of interrogation, leading him into a long, uncontrolled monologue, pitiable in its attempts to justify every aspect of his behaviour:

Take the tow-line – defective equipment, no more, no less, but they encouraged the crew to go round scoffing at me and spreading wild rumours about steaming in circles, and – and then 'Old Yellowstain' – *I* was to blame for Lieutenant Meryk's incompetence and poor seamanship. Lieutenant Meryk was the perfect officer, but not Captain Queeg. Ah, but the strawberries! That's – that's where I had them. They laughed at me and made jokes, but I proved beyond a shadow of a doubt and with – geometric logic that a duplicate key to the ward-room icebox *did* exist, and I'd have produced that key if they hadn't pulled the *Caine* out of action. I – I know now they were only trying to protect some fellow officer, and . . .

Particularly impressive is the naturalism with which he hesitates over, and then homes in on, the word 'geometric', and the shamed, puzzled silence as he breaks off, as if suddenly hearing himself for the first time, before mumbling, 'Naturally, I can only cover these things from memory.' It's a perfectly judged performance – expressive but not theatrical, intense but not histrionic – which earns Bogart a place among the very best screen actors.

Queeg in the courtroom.

6

THE
DESPERATE
HOURS

last films, last days

In celebration of Bogart's performance in *The Caine Mutiny*, *Time* magazine now decided to do a cover story on him, and this was to have an unfortunate effect on his next film, *Sabrina*. It meant that there were reporters hanging around during the shooting, which gave him plentiful opportunities to publicize his dislike of the director, Billy Wilder. The difficulties between the two men were therefore blown up until they assumed the status of a feud. And Maurice Zolotow, Wilder's biographer, has suggested that there might have been another *Caine*-related reason for this development: 'Perhaps Bogart identified too strongly with Queeg while filming *The Caine Mutiny*. He had gone straight from that picture to *Sabrina*. His delusions of persecution seized on anything.'

Bogart's principal anxiety was that Wilder was in cahoots with the co-stars, Audrey Hepburn and William Holden. He was said to be worried that they were getting too many close-ups, and that Wilder was secretly planning for the Holden character to end up with the Hepburn character, leaving Bogart out in the cold. (In a pattern that seems to have haunted his career, the *Sabrina* script was being written at the last minute, although this was not Wilder's usual method at all.) If this behaviour has an uncharacteristic smack of the prima donna, the explanation must be presumed to lie in the distrust and temperamental differences between Bogart and William Holden – who was a

close friend of Wilder's, having been given two of his most worthwhile parts in the director's *Sunset Boulevard* and *Stalag 17*.

Holden was a Republican and a puritan, still happily married to his first wife after thirteen years and famously reluctant to attend Hollywood parties and night-clubs. Bogart was a Democrat, a heavy drinker and compulsive socializer who in 1955 was instrumental in the setting up of the 'Rat Pack', a loose-knit aggregation of drinking buddies and their wives whose activities have achieved some notoriety (partly because they have been described in such detail by some of his biographers, who seem to think that Bogart never did anything more interesting in his life). The Rat Pack was not in existence when *Sabrina* was made, but some comments made by Holden in a 1956 interview vividly illustrate his tight-lipped disapproval of the spirit in which the group was conceived: 'It's terribly important for people to realize that their conduct reflects on the way in which a nation is represented in the eyes of the world . . . It might sound stuffy and dull, but it is quite possible for people to have social intercourse without resorting to a rat pack and even to drink or do anything without resorting to a rat pack . . . People have worked for years to lend some dignity to our profession and it reflects on the community and on my children and on their children and everybody's children.'

This note of piety is light-years away from

With Audrey Hepburn in Sabrina. *'She's all right,' Bogart is supposed to have said, 'if you don't mind a dozen takes.'*

Marlene Dietrich, a close friend of director Billy Wilder, pays a visit to the less than harmonious Sabrina *set.*

any that Bogart ever sounded, but the interesting thing about *Sabrina* is the way it casts Holden as the fast-living reprobate (David Larrabee) and Bogart as his puritanical brother, Linus. Audrey Hepburn, meanwhile, is the chauffeur's daughter, Sabrina Fairchild, for whose attentions they compete during the course of the movie. It is one of Wilder's most treacly concoctions, hampered by a soundtrack that plays interminable variations on 'La Vie en Rose' and 'Isn't It Romantic?' and fatally undermined by a mannered performance by Hepburn, whose gamine-like appeal has dated badly. For the last hour or so Bogart gropes his way through the romantic stodge like a somnambulist, but in the first half – perhaps when he still had some enthusiasm for the project – he seems more attuned than anybody else to the comic spirit of the film. He is particularly good, as might be expected, in a scene where he attempts to woo Sabrina by taking her out sailing. As he regales her with stories about an improbably tragic romantic past, his overplaying is nicely pitched: this is probably the best comic scene he ever did, a cheerful send-up of the wounded-lover image which he had milked mercilessly from *Casablanca* onwards. He is not afraid, either, to cut an undignified figure by dressing up in front of a mirror in some unsuitably youthful sailing togs. 'Look at me,' he says disdainfully. 'Joe College with a touch of arthritis.'

So where did the relationship between

Sending himself up as Linus Larrabee in Sabrina. *'Paris is for lovers . . . Maybe that's why I stayed only thirty-five minutes.'*

Wilder and Bogart go wrong? The agent Swifty Lazar, who was a friend of both men, believed it was simply a clash of titanic egos: 'Bogart was a man of caprices, which Billy did not find amusing. Bogart thought that a director must humble himself before Bogart. On a Billy Wilder picture, there is no star but Billy Wilder.' Wilder was also infuriated – like many other people who worked with Bogart – by his insistence on leaving the set at six o'clock sharp. 'You're all set up for a shot,' he said, 'and it's exactly six p.m. Maybe it took you three hours to light the shot. He will not stay on for ten minutes to finish the shot; he will walk out.' Six o'clock was the time when Bogart promised himself his first glass of Scotch.

Another possible explanation is that Bogart and Wilder were in some respects too similar: both had sadistic, aggressive senses of humour and enjoyed playing on their opponents' weaknesses. Bogart probably came off worse from these exchanges, since, as Wilder put it, 'I learned from the master, Erich von Stroheim, and this is just child's play. I'm in the major leagues.' His remarks about Bogart as an actor are, however, more interesting than most:

'Bogart is a strange mixture of the laziest and the most conscientious actor. He is an extremely competent s.o.b. He comes on the set on time, but completely unprepared. But by the time the lights are set and, having looked at the particular scene about to be shot for a few minutes, he

knows his lines. He never blows them.

'But competent as he is, he is competent only for the bare necessities of a scene. He never learns the complete scene, just the little bit of it that we are photographing from the one camera angle at the time. He has tremendous powers of concentration for short stretches. He doesn't like to cram his mind full of stuff. He knows just bits of a scene at any one time.

'He doesn't study a script at home at all. He

may have a vague conception of what the script is about, but that's all . . . He gives it you in short spurts and it looks like a whole thought out conception when it comes out.'

Bogart and Wilder parted on good terms, but there was never any question of their working together again. This is a shame, because every so often *Sabrina* shows welcome signs of subverting Bogart's traditional persona, and Wilder (whose visual sense is

With Bacall at the Sabrina *première. (Is it a dress, or a raincoat?)*

Strolling around Portofino with Bacall, Ava Gardner and David Hanna (publicist on The Barefoot Contessa).

With Ava Gardner in The Barefoot Contessa. *Yet again, Bogart failed to hit it off with his co-star.*

invariably being underrated by critics) was one of the few directors sufficiently undaunted by Bogart to be able to think of him, occasionally, as no more than a figure in a larger composition – such as in the shot of his tiny silhouette, distantly visible in his lamp-lit office as Audrey Hepburn retreats down a corridor which becomes a block of spreading, impenetrable darkness.

Bogart's next director, Joseph L. Mankiewicz, showed considerably less flair and intelligence when it came to filming *The Barefoot Contessa*. In the fifties this was probably thought of as a handsome and opulent film, but today it seems a flabby exercise in lurid technicolour, moving relentlessly from one expensive location to another so that its very

glamour soon starts to pall. And this in spite of the fact that the story had some promise: Harry Dawes, a washed-up film director (Bogart) attends the funeral of Maria Vargas, a beautiful and enigmatic movie star (Ava Gardner), and tells the audience, in voice-over, the story of how she met her death. (A similar plot and format were used to much better effect in Billy Wilder's *Fedora* twenty-three years later.)

This could have been a powerful role for Bogart, but his lines have no sparkle and there appears to be little chemistry in his relationship with Gardner: off the set, in any case, he made no effort to conceal his dislike of her. Although he regarded it as 'very adult, very exciting' – or at least was willing to say so for

Back home with Bacall, Steve and new daughter Leslie.

publicity purposes – few people nowadays are likely to share this view of a film that is prepared to sacrifice everything on the altar of Mankiewicz's dimestore philosophy. Movies are tidy, life is not – that seems to be the message (in case we didn't know it already), and it is signposted at regular intervals: 'One of the many troubles with you, Harry, is that you never know where your movie scripts leave off and life begins'; 'You're being disloyal, Oscar – you're stealing dialogue from television';

'Once more, life louses up the script', and so on.

Bogart was in Italy for three months to film *The Barefoot Contessa*, just as he had been the previous year for *Beat the Devil*, and Bacall did not accompany him for the whole of either trip, preferring to stay at home to look after the children. (Their daughter, Leslie, had been born on 23 August 1952.) It is during these and other separations that Verita Thompson, Bogart's hairdresser and 'executive secretary', claims to have had her affair with him – an

Bogart, Aldo Ray and Peter Ustinov form an unusual trio of escaped convicts in We're No Angels.

affair that she traces back to 1942. She made
her revelations public in the early 1980s in a
book called *Bogie and Me* (not recommended
for readers with weak stomachs). The possibility that Bogart was unfaithful to Bacall might
have raised interesting questions about the
popular image of the marriage as an extension
of their screen romance, had Thompson stated
her case in a more digestible way. She did,
after all, work and travel extensively with
Bogart, and might have written a revealing
account of his character and working methods.
As it is, though, the tone of her book is too
vindictive – particularly towards Bacall – to in-
spire any confidence in its revelations.

Bogart continued to hunt out different
challenges in his film roles, but the lack of a
guiding hand – even the heavy hand of the
Warners executives – meant that he frequently
ended up working on ill-advised projects.
We're No Angels (1955) wasn't bad. It offered
the chance to work with Michael Curtiz again,
although judging by the pace of the film a
touch of directorial arthritis must have set in
since the far-off days of *Casablanca*. Bogart is
one of a trio of convicts who escape from
Devil's Island in the Christmas of 1895 (the
other two are Peter Ustinov and Aldo Ray –
both splendid). They billet themselves on a
small family, thus paving the way for some
whimsical comedy which derives mostly from
the conflict between this cosy domestic setting
and the crooks' villainous background. 'We

Leo G. Carroll, director Michael
Curtiz and a smiling Bogart welcome
James Cagney to the set of We're
No Angels.

came here to rob them and that's what we're going to do,' says Bogart. 'Beat their heads in. Gouge their eyes out. Cut their throats.' (Pause.) 'As soon as we've washed the dishes.' *We're No Angels* never lets you forget that it's a filmed play, but it's fun all the same.

The same cannot be said of Edward Dmytryk's *The Left Hand of God*, in which Bogart looks distinctly uncomfortable as a World War II pilot disguised, none too convincingly, as a priest. After that came a return to more familiar ground with two parts that took him straight back to the lip-curling, gun-toting days of the 1930s. The first was a new version of *The Petrified Forest*, which went out live on television in May 1955 with Bacall and Henry Fonda in the Bette Davis and Leslie Howard parts. Robert Sherwood stood by in the studio and congratulated them afterwards: nobody seemed to mind that Bogart was by now about twenty years too old to play Duke Mantee. And his third film of 1955, *The Desperate Hours*, was also a throwback to *The Petrified Forest*, with a touch of *Key Largo* thrown in, but without the political overtones of either.

The format of *The Desperate Hours* was by now an over-familiar one – ruthless gunmen hold terrified family hostage in their own home – so perhaps it was simply the impulse to re-orientate himself that led Bogart to take on the flat and unsympathetic role of Glenn Griffin, which he played with robotic efficiency. He had originally wanted to buy the story himself,

With Henry Fonda, rehearsing for the live 1955 television version of The Petrified Forest.

With Lee J. Cobb in The Left Hand
of God. *One of its few claims to
distinction is that it was Bogart's only
Cinemascope film.*

but Paramount outbid him and he ended up agreeing to do the film for only a token fee, largely because he wanted to work with William Wyler again. ('I would have paid Willy to let me do it,' he said.) Frederic March played the father: the part had been intended for Spencer Tracy but, however close his friendship with Bogart, and however much fun it might have been to work together again for the first time in twenty-five years, the two stars couldn't agree about who should get top bill-

ing, and so the deal fell through. It seems you should never underestimate the ego of the Hollywood actor.

Although Bogart had given some good performances in his last nine films, it could be argued that he had not made a really satisfying picture – one in which the script, direction and cast were all worthy of his own contribution – since *The African Queen* back in 1951. Fortunately there was to be one more gem before his career came to its untimely end, and

this was *The Harder They Fall*, a dour exposé of the boxing racket, which is comfortably the best film of its director, Mark Robson.

Not that it has anything especially new to say about its subject: the revelation that boxing is a bloody and corrupt business is essentially no more startling, and needed no more spelling out, than the long-winded message about the futility of greed that John Huston laboured to put across in *The Treasure of the Sierra Madre*. *The Harder They Fall* is best seen

Taking direction from William Wyler during the rehearsals for The Desperate Hours. *The film looks slightly better in the light of the recent Michael Cimino remake.*

With Bacall at the première.

The collision of two different styles: world-weary Bogart and venal Rod Steiger in The Harder They Fall.

as a film about acting, not boxing, and about the collision between two different cinematic styles rather than two prizefighters. At the centre of the movie is a contest between the new, quasi-realistic, Method-influenced performance of Rod Steiger and Bogart's more relaxed and laid-back approach: a contest neatly paralleled in the script itself, which pits Bogart – as the old-fashioned, residually idealistic sportswriter Eddie Willis – against Steiger's fast-talking, flashy and manipulative fight manager. The analogy between boxing and acting is made explicit in a speech where Steiger attempts to persuade Bogart of the

changes that have taken place in the fight business: 'Listen to me, Willis, you've got your sights all screwed up. The fight game today is like show business, there's no real fighters any more, they're all actors. Now you wouldn't hesitate to publicize an actor, would you?'

Robson's direction borrows so shamelessly from every up-to-the-minute cinematic cliché that the film becomes a disarming compendium of fifties styles. The credits zoom on to the screen, white lettering against jagged black cut-outs; Hugo Friedhofer's score is pastiche Bernstein (Leonard and Elmer), saturated with percussion and jazzy inflections; the loca-

tions (windswept streets, deserted warehouses) are chosen for their squalor and the sets (seedy hotel rooms, grimy apartments) for their sleaziness; a jerky hand-held camera is deployed to give immediacy to the fight scenes. And through all of this walks Bogart, thoroughly out of place but at the same time so keenly aware of it that his very presence gives the film a dignity that its hand-me-down methods otherwise fail to earn. Of particular interest is the scene where Steiger makes a lengthy, painfully insincere speech to his fighter Toro Moreno (Mike Lane), attempting to dissuade him from leaving town and going back to his family in South America: time and again we cut away from Steiger's flailing theatrics to a close-up of Willis, watching in silent disbelief, every eye movement and facial tic offering its own eloquent comment on a 'performance' that is wildly at odds with the convictions of both Willis the character and Bogart the actor who plays him.

While Bogart was by no means contemptuous of the Method actors (and Steiger is superb in this film, a powerhouse of shifty, cynical venality), he recognized that their approach was quite foreign to him and made a point of giving several interviews at this time that poked nervous fun at their ascendancy: 'These Actors' Studio types – they mumble their lines. I can't hear their words. I miss the cues . . . This scratch-your-ass-and-mumble school of acting doesn't please me.' He also

A typical Bogart gesture of last-minute nobility: Eddie Willis hands over his earnings to the bruised fighter Toro Moreno.

*Bogie and Bacall arrive at the
Pantages Theatre to find out whether
he has won an Oscar for* The Caine
Mutiny.

said that you should never do a scene with a Method actor that took place at the dinner table, because you would always end up with food all over your clothes. Bogart must have known, all the same, that his own style was on the way out. It was symptomatic of this that in 1951 he had beaten Brando to the Academy Award (*The African Queen* v. *A Streetcar Named Desire*), but in 1954 the situation had been reversed (*On The Waterfront* v. *The Caine Mutiny*). John Huston believed the change was for the better, and said so many years later when discussing his 1975 film, *The Man Who Would Be King*: '. . . the casting of Connery and Caine is indicative of the great changes, thank heavens, which have taken place in the star system and movie-making in general. They bring a reality to it that the old stars, much as I loved Gable and Bogart, could not do . . . Today they would seem synthetic, so in a way I'm glad I didn't make the picture with them.' If the mid-1950s marked a turning-point in American screen acting, *The Harder They Fall* can be seen as a crucial film, making creative use of the Bogart persona (whether intentionally or not is beside the point) to invoke an entire cinematic vocabulary that was beginning to seem radically out of step with the times. In this respect it is eerily appropriate that it should have been his last movie, and that he was to be spared the experience of finding himself overtaken by the new techniques.

But this is speculation – we shall never know for sure. Bogart was preparing himself for two more films, *The Good Shepherd* (from a story by C.S. Forester) and *Melville Goodwin, USA* (in which he was to co-star with Bacall), but neither of them got made. One day in the week after Christmas, 1955, he was having lunch with Greer Garson, who expressed anxiety at the sound of his dry, insistent cough. He told her that he was also off his food, and that his throat had started to burn whenever he drank orange juice. She persuaded him to see a doctor. Cancer of the oesophagus was diagnosed, and on 1 March 1956, he was submitted to a punishing nine-and-a-half-hour operation at the Good Samaritan Hospital. Most of the malignancy was removed, but after having less than a month to recover he was told that an eight-week programme of X-ray treatment would be needed to finish the job. The cumulative effects of tiredness and nausea were far worse than the doctors had predicted, and for a while Bogart was entirely without appetitie. He began to lose weight steadily.

These were blank, dismal weeks, but his sense of humour rarely deserted him, even in the face of tastelessly exaggerated press reports about his condition. One reporter claimed that he was fighting for his life in the 'Memorial Hospital' in Los Angeles, when there wasn't any such place – prompting Bogart to fire off this rejoinder: 'I have read that both lungs have been removed; that I couldn't live another half-hour; that I was fighting for my life in a hospital which doesn't exist out here; that my heart has stopped and been replaced by an old gasoline pump from a defunct Standard Oil station. I have been on the way to practically every cemetery from here to the Mississippi – including several where I am certain they only accept dogs. All the above upsets my friends, not to mention the insurance companies . . .'

His friends were certainly upset, not only by the newspaper stories but by the visible deterioration in his condition, which was even worse after another visit to the hospital for nitrogen mustard treatment (scar tissue had formed after the surgery, pressing upon a nerve in his left shoulder and causing him terrible pain). Eventually Bogart was too weak to walk, and either had to receive visitors in his bedroom or would make use of the dumb waiter to carry him downstairs, where he liked to sit for an hour every evening with one or two of his closest friends – the Nivens, Frank Sinatra, Nunnally Johnson and wife, Spencer Tracy and Katharine Hepburn, a few others. Lauren Bacall, who has described this period in moving and exhaustive detail in her autobiography, was in constant attendance: a friend of Bogart's is said to have reminded him that she had hardly had a single evening out in the last ten months, to which he answered: 'She's my wife and my nurse. So she stays home. Maybe

Family portrait taken in August 1954.

that's the way you tell the ladies from the broads in this town.'

However much she did for him, she was powerless to stop the disease, and Bogart died in a coma in the early hours of 14 January 1957.

In the eulogy that he delivered at the funeral three days later, John Huston pointed out that Bogart's life, although rich and full, was 'not a long one measured in years'. Even briefer, though, was the period of his real success: fifteen years at the height of his profession, after more than four decades of struggles, setbacks, false starts, miscalculations, failed marriages, failed films, frustrations, unhappiness. It is the history of these forty years that we read on Bogart's face in *Casablanca*, in the awesome unflappability of Harry Morgan in *To Have and Have Not* and of Philip Marlowe in *The Big Sleep*. The weight of his experience, and the energy and intelligence with which he sometimes – not always – brought it to the screen, coalesced into a personality bigger than cinema itself. If, from the 1940s onwards, he looked uncomfortable and constrained in genre pictures such as *Dead Reckoning* and *Dark Passage*, this was because he had not simply outgrown the genre but had created a genre of his own. To the gangster movie, the private-eye movie, the women's picture and the *film noir* we now have to add the 'Bogart movie', a genre that by definition could admit of only one practitioner. Not everything about it was admirable: the impatience and authority of his persona could shade into sadism, the cynicism into self-pity, and these undersides may well have been part of the man as well as his screen creation. You can try to do justice to Bogart's influence simply by recognizing his impact on the cinema, from the overt *hommages* of *À Bout de Souffle*, *Gumshoe* and *Play It Again, Sam* right down to the efforts of any actor who ever tried to put flesh and feeling on to the underwritten part of a cheap detective; but this would be to forget that the films and the life were, in Bogart's case, entangled – perhaps more thoroughly and more messily than with any other Hollywood star. Arguments over his personal qualities will continue to recede helplessly into history, but it remains true that nobody walks out of one of the great Bogart movies without having seen something that uplifts and enriches. Without having *learned* something, in fact, because if his career and his films provide equal cause for celebration, it is because they teach us a strategy, and a very wholesome one, for dealing with life at its best and its worst. Take it and like it.

FILMOGRAPHY

Feature Films

1930	A Devil with Women
	Up the River

1931 Body and Soul
Bad Sister
Women of all Nations
A Holy Terror

1932 Love Affair
Big City Blues
Three on a Match

1934 Midnight

1936 The Petrified Forest
Bullets or Ballots
Two Against the World
China Clipper
Isle of Fury

1937 Black Legion
The Great O'Malley
Marked Woman
Kid Galahad
San Quentin
Dead End
Stand-In
Swing Your Lady

1938 Crime School
Men Are Such Fools
The Amazing Dr Clitterhouse
Racket Busters
Angels with Dirty Faces

1939 King of the Underworld
The Oklahoma Kid
You Can't Get Away with Murder
Dark Victory
The Roaring Twenties
The Return of Doctor X
Invisible Stripes

1940 Virginia City
It All Came True
Brother Orchid
They Drive by Night

1941 High Sierra
The Wagons Roll at Night
The Maltese Falcon

1942 All Through the Night
The Big Shot
Across the Pacific
Casablanca

1943 Action in the North Atlantic
Sahara

1944 Passage to Marseille
To Have and Have Not

1945 Conflict

1946 The Big Sleep

1947 Dead Reckoning
The Two Mrs Carrolls
Dark Passage

1948 The Treasure of the Sierra Madre
Key Largo

1949 Knock on Any Door
Tokyo Joe

1950 Chain Lightning
In a Lonely Place

1951 The Enforcer
Sirocco
The African Queen

1952 Deadline USA

1953 Battle Circus
Beat the Devil

1954 The Caine Mutiny
Sabrina
The Barefoot Contessa

1955 We're No Angels
The Left Hand of God

The Desperate Hours

1956 The Harder They Fall

Shorts

The Dancing Town (1928)
Broadway's Like That (1930)
Report from the Front (1944)
Hollywood Victory Caravan (1945)
US Savings Bond Trailer (1952)

Guest Appearances

In This Our Life (1942)
Thank Your Lucky Stars (1943)
Two Guys from Milwaukee (1946)
Always Together (1947)
The Love Lottery (1954)

ACKNOWLEDGEMENTS

AP/WIDE WORLD PHOTOS, New York
AQUARIUS PICTURE LIBRARY, Hastings
ASSOCIATED PRESS, London
BETTMANN ARCHIVE, New York
CULVER PICTURES, New York
RONALD GRANT ARCHIVE, London
PHILIPPE HALSMAN/MAGNUM PHOTOS, London
DARLENE HAMMOND/RETNA PICTURES, London
HULTON-DEUTSCH, London
KATZ PICTURES, London
KOBAL COLLECTION, London
POPPERFOTO, London
SNAP-PHOTO, Hollywood
DENNIS STOCK/MAGNUM PHOTOS, London
TOPHAM PICTURE SOURCE, Kent
UPI/BETTMANN ARCHIVE, New York

BFI STILLS, POSTERS AND DESIGN, London, with
acknowledgement to COLUMBIA, FOX, PARAMOUNT,
TWENTIETH CENTURY-FOX, UNITED ARTISTS,
WARNER BROTHERS